London's 100 Best Churches

LEIGH HATTS

CANTERBURY
PRESS
Norwich

xt and photography © Leigh Hatts 2010

First published in 2010 by the Canterbury Press Norwich
Editorial office
13–17 Long Lane,
London, EC1A 9PN, UK

Canterbury Press is an imprint of Hymns Ancient and Modern Ltd (a registered charity)
St Mary's Works, St Mary's Plain,
Norwich, NR3 3BH, UK

www.scm-canterburypress.co.uk

British Library Cataloguing in Publication data

A catalogue record for this book is available
from the British Library

978 1 84811 944 6

Typeset by Regent Typesetting, London
Printed and bound in Great Britain by
Ashford Colour Press Ltd, Gosport, Hants

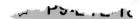

Contents

Preface

'Churches are the spiritual background to our whole country,' said Jools Holland when supporting the *Sunday Telegraph* 'Save Our Churches' campaign. 'Churches aren't touchy-feely headphone and flatscreen experiences, they are real life, they are where our ancestors lie.'

Frank Field MP added: 'Historic buildings tell us something about the past, link us to the past, and hopefully take us into the future.'

There are recurring names of architects and clergy in the story of London's churches. Britain's two favourite poets, T. S. Eliot and John Donne, are both found deeply involved in parish life.

The turning point for the City, the Great Fire of 1666, allowed Christopher Wren to introduce to the churches of the City of London a new simplicity that has adapted so well.

The spreading influence of Anglo-Catholicism, also known as the Oxford Movement or Catholic Anglicanism, can be seen in the history of London's Victorian churches. Here too can be found the eventual flowering of church music to the benefit of congregations far beyond the capital.

The Bishop of London has described the recent restoration of St George's in Bloomsbury as 'part of the Church's recognition of its own responsibilities in London and in the nation in a situation where pointing the finger at others is inadequate' when evoking the energy for the transformation of moral values.

His predecessor David Hope, preaching in 2009 at All Saints in Margaret Street, thanked God for churches that are freely open for all who seek to enter them: 'Here you are assured that the Lord loves you.'

London is so rich in churches that choosing the best 100 at first seemed daunting. A church does not have to be an architectural masterpiece to be interesting and worth visiting.

However, some great buildings with resonance failed to qualify by being closed all week apart from a service, sometimes just the Sunday service, as in the case of The Annunciation, Marble Arch. As a result of rising crime it is no longer possible to drop into St John the Divine in Kennington where Michael Ramsey chose to celebrate his last Eucharist as Primate. But opening churches on weekdays is a trend, especially in the City and West End, and this is encouraged by Ecclesiastical

Insurance which believes that a used building is better protected than one that is ignored all day.

All the churches featured here are, except for Hampstead Church's Roman Catholic neighbour, either open daily or at a regular time in addition to services, so enabling visitors to enter without the fear of being trapped in unaccustomed worship.

But a church only displays a complete face when its congregation is gathered for the main weekly service. Those who do choose to join in worship in any one of the 100 churches may find not just great architecture, art, music and liturgy but even a good preacher. In central London, church attendance has grown during the last decade so more often than not there will be a faithful and even quietly growing congregation.

The book's website, www.londons100bestchurches.co.uk, provides the latest opening times and information on services.

I am, of course, grateful for the welcome and help I have received from many clergy, vergers and church watchers.

Leigh Hatts
November 2009

London's 100 Best Churches

I
St Alban's, Holborn
Anglican

This Anglo-Catholic shrine is hidden behind High Holborn's huge Prudential headquarters designed by Alfred Waterhouse. War damage has left the church with an awesome interior of simplicity.

The building was first designed by William Butterfield and opened in 1863 as the church of a new parish carved out of St Andrew's in Holborn. It was a small area with a population of 8,000 poor people. The saddleback roof and the tower were inspired by St Kunibert's in Cologne, which was also to suffer war damage. The entrance is through an archway beneath the integral clergy house.

The church was paid for by a former Bank of England governor, John Hubbard MP, who became the first Lord Addington.

The nave and sanctuary were remodelled by Adrian Scott and consecrated in 1961. The original cross and candlesticks are on the high altar. But dominating the church's east end is a 60-foot-high mural of the *Trinity in Glory* by Hans Feibusch. His stations of the cross are down the sides of the church.

The first vicar was Alexander Mackonochie, who was hugely influential in promoting the catholic tradition not only here but also in many other parishes. In 1865 he introduced the Three Hours Service on Good Friday, which was gradually adopted by other churches. Behind his effigy in the Mackonochie Chapel are portrayed the two dogs who watched over his body when he died alone on a snow-covered Scottish mountain. His curate, Arthur Stanton, stayed in Holborn for 50 years and has a tomb chest memorial in the church.

The prolific Victorian novelist Adeline Sergeant helped with mission work here among young women, and later Sir Reginald Goodall was director of music.

The school on the north side was founded before the church. There is of course no churchyard, but twice a year the congregation goes to its burial ground, complete with lychgate, at Brookwood in Surrey where Fr Mackonochie and Fr Stanton are buried. For summer breaks from the city, there was until 2008 a parish seaside holiday home in Kent.

Since 1992 the church's north aisle has run directly into a glazed cloister giving access to the award-winning St Alban's Centre, which is both a community and conference centre. It was here that the movement Affirming Catholicism had its foundation meeting.

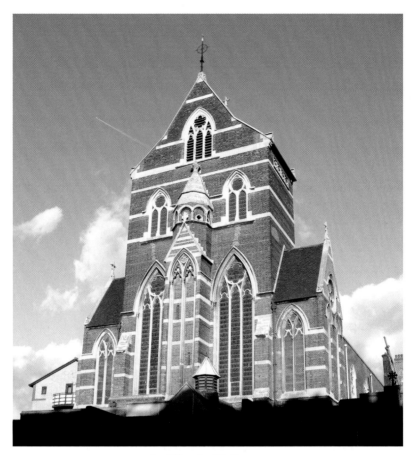
St Alban's, Holborn

The present St Alban's ethos owes much to its eighth vicar, John Gaskell, who was here in the 1980s and made it a church for everyone. It is both a parish church and a shrine to refresh those ministering and worshipping far away in less inspiring parishes.

St Alban's probably has the highest standard of liturgy anywhere in London. Mass is said daily in the Mackonochie Chapel and on Sunday there is a Sung Mass and a Solemn Mass. A professional choir performs the great Mass settings and premieres new works.

Hans Feibusch's 1985 sculpture *Jesus Raised From The Dead* greets visitors in the courtyard. It was his last work for the parish.

Open lunchtimes Monday to Friday
Brooke Street EC1N 7RD
www.stalbans-holborn.com

2

All Hallows-by-the-Tower, Tower Hill
Anglican

All Hallows stands on Tower Hill above its neighbour, the Tower of London. The church, with its distinctive seventeenth-century tower, topped by a green postwar spire, now forms not just the City approach to the fortress but the north side of Tower Place piazza which is dominated by a twenty-first-century financial development.

Inside, the wide nave is light with a focus on a fifteenth-century altarpiece. The statues of St James the Great and St Roche are 500 years old. The sense of space survives the presence of numerous monuments and an extensive bookstall. Below there is a crypt with traces of a Roman pavement.

Barking Abbey founded this church in the Saxon period, which makes it not only the City's oldest church but older than the Tower of London, begun by William the Conqueror. However, the Tower has dominated the church's history, with the headless bodies of those executed on Tower Green often being brought here. Among them was St Thomas More and Archbishop Laud. Another was St John Fisher, who has recently been commemorated with an icon triptych by Michael Coles.

The font has an extraordinary limewood cover carved by Grinling Gibbons. Baptisms include Bishop Lancelot Andrewes, who now lies across the river in Southwark Cathedral, and the founder of Pennsylvania, William Penn. His father saved the church from the Great Fire of 1666 by having houses in the path of the flames pulled down and, with Samuel Pepys, he watched the fire's progress from the tower.

Among those married here are Judge Jeffreys, whose victims died at nearby Wapping, and American President John Quincy Adams.

A famous vicar from 1922 to 1963 was Tubby Clayton, founder of TocH, who is buried where the TocH lamp burns as a symbol of the light of Christ. It was during his ministry that the church was hit by a bomb and restored by architect Lord Mottistone, who revealed the Anglo-Saxon work.

Peter Delaney, vicar, archdeacon and artist, arrived in 1977 and did much to revitalize the church as part of the diverse business community. He was also responsible for reviving beating the bounds on Ascension Day, which involves both visiting the parish boundary in the Thames by boat and meeting the Beefeaters on the Liberty of the Tower boundary.

All Hallows-by-the-Tower, Tower Hill

This church is part of the tourist trail and hosts the London Marathon service held the night before the runners pass the door. But it also has both a weekday and a Sunday congregation made up of people from many countries. Its international ministry includes being a meeting place for the Friends of the Diocese of Cyprus and the Gulf. The church's American associations are continued by a twinning with The Epiphany in New York.

The main entrance from Byward Street was only built in the 1880s but the creation of the new piazza may mean that once again the south door away from the traffic is the most used.

Open weekdays 8am to 6pm; weekends 10am to 5pm
Byward Street EC3R 5BJ
www.ahbtt.org.uk

3
All Saints, Fulham

Anglican

The landmark tower is of similar style and age to that of St Mary's in Putney, at the opposite end of Putney Bridge. Both feature in the annual Boat Race television coverage. Like Putney's church, Fulham's was also rebuilt in the nineteenth century.

All Saints stands in a pleasant setting behind double gates. At the churchyard's inland gate there are charming gothic-style Sir William Powell Almshouses, designed by J. P. Seddon and completed in 1870. The backdrop to both church and almshouses are the rural grounds of the once moated Fulham Palace where the Bishop of London lived for many centuries until 1973.

The first church here was probably built in the thirteenth century, although there is a twelfth-century font in the churchyard which may point to an early chapel. Certainly the Bishops of London had held the manor since the year 704. The nearby Parsons Green Station takes its name from the vicarage.

In 1880 the church, with the exception of the tower which has a fourteenth-century base, was rebuilt to designs by Sir Arthur Blomfield, who placed the east window – given 40 years earlier by his father, Bishop Blomfield – in the south transept.

Among the many memorials transferred from the demolished nave which often flooded is a memorial to Henry VIII's doctor, Sir William Butts, who features in Shakespeare's play *Henry VIII*. Another recalls Henry's painter Master Gerard Hornebolt's wife Margaret, who is buried here.

Naturally, London bishops are associated with this church and several lie in a row outside, including Thomas Sherlock who died in 1761, having remodelled parts of the palace. Also buried outside the vestry door is architect Henry Holland. To the west of the church is a 1999 sculpture called *Mother and Child* by Helen Sinclair.

Today, thousands walk past the church to and from Fulham Football Club's riverside Craven Cottage ground. Glass doors allow a clear view into the church.

The church maintains a ministry of welcome with office holders including, as well as the expected churchwardens and sidespeople, cellarers to ensure adequate drinks for social occasions. Newlywed couples are offered a special peal of bells as enjoyed by Elizabeth I when passing on the river. In 1629 six old tower bells were

Almshouses alongside All Saints, Fulham

recast along with two new ones, which explains the name given to the Eight Bells pub in Fulham High Street.

There is a high standard of music, and just before the millennium the congregation here was considered representative enough to be chosen to trial the Common Worship texts now adopted by the Church of England. This is a church where the rhythm of the year is maintained with the blessing of the allotments at Rogation and tower-top singing early on Ascension Day.

On Sundays there is both a Sung Eucharist and a very well-attended Family Eucharist. All Saints has three choirs: one to sing Choral Evensong on Sundays, a 40-strong junior one, and a gospel choir.

Open Monday to Friday 10am to 3pm
Bishops Park SW6 3LA
www.allsaints-fulham.org.uk

4
All Saints, Margaret Street
Anglican

The 227-foot spire, seen by shoppers leaving the Marks & Spencer Pantheon branch in Oxford Street, is a reminder of William Butterfield's finest church hidden in a side street.

The Margaret Street Chapel opened on the site in 1760. Within a century, when William Gladstone attended, it was rebuilt in brick to be a model for the Oxford Movement. The foundation stone was laid in 1850 by Dr Edward Pusey and today 'Margaret Street' remains the flagship Anglo-Catholic church.

'It was here, in the 1850s, that the revolution in architecture began,' said Sir John Betjeman. Simon Jenkins calls it 'England's most intriguing Victorian church'. Bookseller Tim Waterstone has spoken of the calm found here: 'It's a privilege for those of us who have found the place, and pray there. I am blessed to be one of them.' Novelist P. D. James features it in *The Murder Room*.

The church, completed in 1859, is found beyond a gabled gate and a courtyard flanked by clergy residences. The interior decoration owes much to John Ruskin's ideas. On the floor are Minton tiles. A late addition by Butterfield is the tiled north wall depicting Old Testament figures and saints around a now much reproduced nativity scene. This was once featured on the Queen's Christmas broadcast.

The fittings were chosen by Butterfield, who preferred simple furnishing but produced a gorgeous highly coloured pulpit. The 1877 west window, designed by Alexander Gibbs, is based on the 'Tree of Jesse' window in Wells Cathedral.

The reredos was completed by William Dyce in 1853–9, but had to be radically restored on new wooden panels by Comper in 1909. He designed the silver pyx which was given by the Duke of Newcastle, churchwarden, in memory of choristers killed in World War One.

All Saints' entrance

Incumbents include William Upton Richards, who was appointed to the old chapel in 1847 and became the first vicar; and, more recently, Michael Marshall who left to be Bishop of Woolwich, and David Hope, who became Archbishop of York.

All Saints, Margaret Street

Former choirmasters include William Lloyd Webber, father of Andrew and Julian. Although its choir school, attended by Laurence Olivier, closed in 1968, there is still a very high standard of music. The 1910 four-manual Harrison and Harrison organ has been restored and there is an impressive list not just of Mass settings, but a 70-strong collection of Benediction settings.

Before St Paul's Cathedral started hosting the Diocesan Eucharist towards the end of the twentieth century, All Saints was a substitute cathedral for central London clergy gathered on Maundy Thursday for the Chrism Mass.

The Sunday Solemn Mass is the main service, followed almost whatever the weather by refreshments in the courtyard. There is also daily Mass as well as celebrations on major festivals. Holy Week is a highlight, when at the climax on Holy Saturday the Easter candle is placed in a candlestick that is a copy of the one at the monastery at Pavia in Italy.

Children are welcomed with colouring books and crayons.

Open 7am to 7pm
Margaret Street W1W 8JG
www.allsaintsmargaretstreet.org.uk

5
All Souls, Langham Place
Anglican

The stone church on the bend in the road is well known for being the focus at the climax of Regent Street and alongside Broadcasting House. Recently the church has become the foil to the BBC Newscentre behind in All Souls Place. The church interior is light but has rich gilding and Corinthian pillars.

All Souls was consecrated in November 1824 following the architect John Nash taking immense care for over a decade with the design. The circular portico allows

All Souls' architect, John Nash

the church to look towards passers-by from either north or south. However, a cartoon still depicted Nash impaled on the spire which was described in the House of Commons as an 'extinguisher on a flat candlestick'. A bust of the architect placed in the portico in 1956 looks down Regent Street.

Above the altar, but sometimes half hidden by a projection screen, is a painting of Christ by Queen Victoria's drawing teacher, Richard Westall. It was given by George IV who had been delighted with the new Regent Street created by Nash to link his Carlton House on The Mall with Regent's Park.

Gerald Priestland described the inside as being like the 'state ballroom of a Regency mansion'. The church was drawn by Eric Fraser for the Holy Week 1980 cover of the *Radio Times*. From 1951 to 1994 the Radio 4 *Daily Service* came live from here and occasionally featured the sound of traffic or drilling. Once it even had to compete with 'Colonel Bogey' being played in front of Broadcasting House by striking musicians.

The many broadcasts have included the memorial service for the BBC's chief announcer Stuart Hibberd in 1983 when a lesson was read by John Snagge.

In 1967 the launch of Radio 1 was marked by the famous group photograph, taken on the steps, of the new DJs – which included Pete Murray, Tony Blackburn, Jimmy Young, Bob Holness and Terry Wogan. In the centre is Mike Raven who reinvented himself as Christian artist Churton Fairman and exhibited at St Paul's Cathedral.

All Souls, Langham Place

John Stott, who was curate and rector for 30 years until 1975, knew the church as a child. His successor was Michael Baughen, the future Bishop of Chester, who re-ordered the chancel and masterminded an excavation below the building to create a hall.

Noel Tredinnick, noted conductor of orchestras and choirs and a familiar face with a baton on BBC1's *Songs of Praise*, has had a strong influence as the director of music. The All Souls Orchestra sometimes plays at services.

In 2008 a rally of the embryo Fellowship of Confessing Anglicans was addressed here by the Archbishops of Uganda and Sydney while stewards held back the gay activist Peter Tatchell.

This is a highly successful church in the evangelical tradition, with a Sunday service followed by lunch, weekday lunchtime talks relayed to the porch, and a large outreach team for shops and businesses.

Open daily
Langham Place W1B 3DA
www.allsouls.org

6

St Andrew's, Holborn

Anglican

St Andrew's is on the fringe of the City in Holborn Circus where the focus is the church tower, which features in both Charles Dickens' *Oliver Twist* and Iris Murdoch's *Under the Net*.

It is a wide and light church but the first building was a wooden Saxon structure above the River Fleet valley. In Norman times it was called St Andrew Holburnestrate, and by 1291 a more substantial building was known as St Andrew de Holeburn. The church survived the Great Fire when the wind changed but it was rebuilt anyway by Wren and is his largest City church. However, the fifteenth-century tower was retained and this also escaped the bomb that destroyed the nave in 1941.

The present Holborn building opened in 1961 and many of the furnishings are from the Foundling Hospital Chapel that stood in nearby Coram's Fields. Also now at St Andrew's is the tomb of its founder, Captain Thomas Coram, who engaged the support of artist William Hogarth, and also Handel, whose *Messiah* was performed to raise money. The Royal Free Hospital was founded in nearby Greville Street after local doctor William Marsden discovered a young girl dying on the steps of the church and was unable to find her a bed.

The many weddings that have taken place here include Lord Chief Justice Coke who in 1598 married 'the Lady of Bleeding Heart Yard', Sir Christopher Hatton's widow. In 1799 engineer Marc Brunel married Sophia Kingdom, who gave birth to railway engineer Isambard Kingdom Brunel. In 1809 Charles Lamb was best man, and his sister Mary was bridesmaid, at the wedding of essayist William Hazlitt.

Henry VIII was a godparent when the Earl of Southampton was baptized. Two Prime Ministers, Henry Addington and, as a teenager, Benjamin Disraeli, were christened here.

The church was once at the top of steps but is now at the bottom due to the raising of the main road in 1869 for building the approach to Holborn Viaduct spanning the River Fleet valley. At the time the opportunity was taken to widen the main road and the loss of the churchyard resulted in 12,000 bodies being removed to Ilford. So poet Thomas Chatterton, who died in his nearby Brooke Street garret in 1770, now lies in East London.

The church, now looking to serve Holborn again, was for a time in the 1990s the

St Andrew's, Holborn

headquarters of the Royal College of Organists. The model is St Gervais in Paris which attempts to bring contemplation to the world of work. This includes good liturgy and a ministry of hospitality. A re-landscaping of the remaining churchyard is taking place and the west door is being re-opened as the main entrance for prayer and worship.

The last lingering bodies have recently been removed from the crypt so it can become a centre for occupational health services, with spare meeting rooms and a quiet candlelit space for reflection.

Open Monday to Friday 9am to 5pm
Holborn Circus EC4A 3AB
www.standrewholborn.org.uk

7
St Andrew's, Totteridge
Anglican

This American-looking church is on high ground where the old lane from Barnet joins the village street at a double bend. There is a tithe barn in front of the church which has an ancient yew tree in its churchyard. The church interior is simple but darker than intended due to the gradual installation of Victorian glass.

There was a church on the site in 1250 dedicated to St Etheldreda. This is because it was on land owned by the Bishop of Ely where the patroness is Etheldreda. The Totteridge estate was a stopping-off point for the regular journey from his Hatfield residence to his Holborn residence (see St Etheldreda's, page 62). The pulpit comes from St Etheldreda's Church at Hatfield. St Etheldreda is also known as St Audrey, and after the Reformation this was mistakenly transcribed here as Andrew.

The existing church was built in 1790 although the weatherboarded bell turret with a weathervane was erected in 1706. A monument in the aisle dated 1711 comes from the earlier building.

The village was part of the Lincoln Diocese until 1845, then briefly in an expanded Rochester Diocese, but since 1877 it has been under the St Albans Diocese despite being also within a London borough. However, St Andrew's remains a daughter church of Hatfield whose rector is the patron.

St Andrew's did not become a parish church until 1892 when the Queen Anne-style vicarage was built. It was the first commission for local architect Sir Charles Nicholson whose wife decorated the chancel roof in 1899. His father, the first baronet and the first Speaker of New South Wales Legislative Council, is remembered with a window designed by another son, Archibald Nicholson.

In 1808 Cardinal Henry Manning was born opposite the church in a now demolished house. His father William was a churchwarden and Henry was prepared for confirmation here and later tutored by the curate. In 1815 the family moved to Kent but Henry, who became an Anglican archdeacon before converting to Rome at Farm Street (see page 64), visited the church when a cardinal. His father and brother are buried under a holly tree behind the church.

Also buried here, in a churchyard with delightful chest tombs, are Sir Lucas Pepys, George III's doctor; Charles Pepys, who as Lord Cottenham was Queen Victoria's first Lord Chancellor; Sir William Peat, George V's accountant in whose memory the unusual altar frontal was given in 1936; and championship golfer

St Andrew's, Totteridge

Harry Vardon. Lord Hewart, Lord Chief Justice who lived opposite at Garden Hill, married here in 1929.

This is a rare surviving rural setting for a church within Greater London. The parish includes meadows and Ellern Mede Farm selling honey and eggs.

Totteridge is known for its famous and wealthy residents but the congregation is still diverse enough to need a Sunday school and crèche. There are daily services and children from the school walk to church on special days.

Open daily 9am to 5pm
Totteridge N20 8PR
www.totteridge.church.btinternet.co.uk

8
St Andrew-by-the-Wardrobe, Blackfriars

Anglican

This curiously named church is found in an alleyway off St Andrew's Hill behind a wine bar disguised as a bookshop. It can also be seen from Queen Victoria Street where the church is at the top of a steep wooded bank above Puddle Dock.

St Andrew's has a clever vestibule running across the west end which allows the church to be seen by visitors through glass even when the main church and chapel are locked. Hanging from the gallery are several banners including the crowned maiden crest of Mercers' Company, the church's patron.

The church's name has intrigued many across the world who until 1964 used to see on the back page of *The Times* the words 'printed and published in the parish of St Andrew-by-the-Wardrobe'. The wardrobe was a building that stood to the north of the church from 1361 until the Great Fire consumed both in 1666. This was the King's store for such items as spare chess sets and state robes. William Shakespeare, who lived in Ireland Yard, visited the wardrobe to collect cloth for costumes and his players were fitted out there in 1604 for their coronation costumes. Wardrobe Place off nearby medieval Carter Lane recalls the lost building.

The church was rebuilt after the Great Fire although it was one of the last to be attended to. Before World War Two the Sunday congregation was largely drawn from across the river and included future Foreign Secretary George Brown who lived in Peabody Square, and the Clewer Sisters whose London house was off Blackfriars Road.

In 1940 an incendiary bomb left only the tower and church walls standing. It was just over 20 years before the rebuild was completed under the direction of Marshall Sisson who used Wren's plans and brought a window from Bulstrode Park House in Buckinghamshire for the east end.

A leading figure in seeing the church restored was the author and MP Ivor Bulmer-Thomas who was churchwarden for 37 years. He is commemorated in the entrance by a memorial window featuring another church saved by him, St John's in Smith Square.

On a windowsill halfway up the gallery stairs is the figure of St Nicholas which was once above the gateway of nearby St Nicholas Cole Abbey.

St Andrew-by-the-Wardrobe, Blackfriars

A picture of Charles I is a reminder that here the Society of King Charles the Martyr marks the King's birthday every November. St Andrew is the church of the Society of Apothecaries whose nearby hall is on the site of Blackfriars monastery. The annual beating the bounds, which includes the Millennium Bridge, serves as a reminder of how the parish now embraces a wider area including that of the St Ann's parish where the church was not rebuilt after the Great Fire. On St Anne's Day, 26 July, there is a procession to the church site in Ireland Yard for an outdoor Eucharist.

Open weekdays
St Andrew's Hill EC4V 5DE
www.standrewbythewardrobe.net

9
St Anne and St Agnes, Aldersgate

Lutheran

The church in Aldersgate is a small brick building with clear glass windows hidden behind a garden in Gresham Street. To find it you must look for the line of taxis attracted by the cafe next door. The interior is small and intimate with nave pews just five deep. The freestanding altar is placed in front of the communion rails. Through the east window the view is of a new City building.

A Norman church, first called St Agnes near Alderychgate and later St Anne-in-the-Willows, had been rebuilt shortly after a fire in 1548 when the congregation numbered 300. This replacement was in turn consumed by the 1666 Great Fire of London. The present building opened in 1680 and was erected under the direction of Christopher Wren who may have left the detailed work to Hooke. Most interesting, in view of the church's present congregation, is a claim that they may have been influenced by a Lutheran church, Nieuwe Kerk, in Haarlem in the Netherlands.

World War Two damage in 1940 led to the issuing of a Dangerous Structure Notice which was ignored by the verger who still admitted visitors. But the diocese seriously considered restoring the brick box not as a church but as a residence for the Bishop of London.

The first mention of a joint dedication bringing Anne and Agnes together was in 1457 when the church called itself SS Anne & Agnes within Aldrichesgate. In 1933 the church had an international focus when the new rector Basil Batty also held the new post of Bishop of Fulham with responsibility for Anglican churches all over Europe.

In 1966 the church became home to the Lutheran congregation which has restored the church to be as Wren knew it with furnishing from lost City churches. The lectern is a charming standing angel dating from about 1900.

More than 30 nationalities worship here with services held in English, Amharic, Estonian, Latvian and Swahili. The congregation has a high proportion of Americans and young people: refreshments often feature chocolate brownies and cookies. The large attendance is accommodated by extra side seating which creates the feel of worship in the round. But there is a high turnover of people owing to the nature of jobs in the financial sector.

This is the only church in the British Isles to offer a regular Bach Vespers. The

St Anne and St Agnes, Aldersgate

tradition was started in 1982 by the minister Ronald Englund and the director of music Peter Lea-Cox. Anglican clergy warned that no one would turn up but the average attendance is over 125. 'Emotionally the music is ungraspable,' Peter Lea-Cox once claimed. 'You unwrap a layer and there's another one. The music's enduring qualities are a sort of miracle.'

In July there is a Bach Festival which is another legacy of the former director of music whose Lecosoldi Ensemble has often performed here. Lunchtime concerts are a regular feature and occasionally there is Jazz Vespers.

Open Monday to Friday 10.30am to 2pm
Gresham Street EC2V 7BX
www.stanneslutheranchurch.org

St Anne's, Kew Green

Anglican

This early seventeenth-century church stands on Kew Green as a backdrop to cricket matches. Although not one of the Royal Chapels, it was used as one over several generations.

The church was built in 1714 on land given by Queen Anne. This building, a chapel in the Kingston parish, was greatly enlarged in 1770 at the expense of King George III who lived at Kew Palace when not in London. The plans were drawn up by Queen Charlotte's drawing teacher John Kirby. Parish status was granted by the Diocese of Winchester, which then embraced Surrey, in 1788.

The portico with its Tuscan columns, the bell tower and cupola all date from William IV's patronage and are the work of Sir William Wyatville. Alterations in 1884 established the size of the present building although the 1902 vestries in memory of Queen Victoria were the basis for the discreet addition of the 1978 church hall.

The church interior is very light thanks to tall windows. The royal gallery was added in 1805 for George III. There are memorials to both Sir William Hooker and his son Sir Joseph who were both Directors of the Royal Botanical Gardens.

The semi-domed mausoleum tacked on the east end was added in 1851 for the burial of the Duke of Cambridge and his wife. Their bodies were moved to Windsor in 1930, leaving the small building to be used for the burial of ashes.

The Duke, George III's youngest son, was known for his excessive participation in the services. His response to the clergyman intoning 'Let us pray' was to reply 'By all means'. His stage whisper during the reading of the Ten Commandments included the aside: 'Quite right but very difficult sometimes!' One curate felt compelled to resign rather than endure such interruptions.

His daughter Princess Mary married here in 1866 after the Duke of Teck proposed in Kew Gardens. The wedding was attended by Queen Victoria, and their daughter Mary became Queen Mary, consort of George V.

The raised churchyard on three sides holds the graves of artists George Gainsborough and Johan Zoffany. The latter's painting of *The Last Supper*, intended for this church, is now found in Brentford Church after the artist modelled Judas on a Kew churchwarden.

Thomas Morrell, sub-curate-in-charge in the 1730s, wrote the libretto for

St Anne's, Kew Green

Handel's *Judas Maccabeus*. A familiar figure assisting at services during World War Two was retired Archbishop of Canterbury Cosmo Gordon Lang.

Easter Day evensong in 1951 was the first Easter service ever to be televised. Today the church seeks to maintain a 'well-ordered choral liturgy' at its Sunday Sung Eucharist celebrated at a facing altar. There is a junior church to take care of the many children who come with their families. In summer, cream teas are served on Sunday afternoons.

Open 9am to noon, except Thursday when the hours are 1pm to 3pm
Kew Green TW9 3AB
www.saintanne-kew.org.uk

II

St Anne's, Limehouse

Anglican

The Portland stone lantern tower, which has the highest church clock in London, is a landmark for shipping on the River Thames. The White Ensign flies from the top both day and night.

It is also seen from many points inland and by passengers on the Docklands Light Railway who have a raised view across the churchyard from the south.

St Anne's was built between 1712 and 1724 with the steeple being completed by 1719. The church had been furnished by 1725 but it was a further five years before it opened. So much had been spent on the magnificent building designed by Nicholas Hawksmoor that there was no money left to pay a priest.

The dedication is to St Anne in recognition of Queen Anne whose approval of the Fifty New Churches Act led to the building of this church. However, the planned statue of the Queen had to be dropped on grounds of cost.

The western entrance, like the front door of a country house, has a beautiful stone vestibule with double doors on two sides.

Inside there is a gallery on three sides with the restored organ at the west end. The east end has recently been re-ordered, with the sanctuary returned to its original level and the nineteenth-century altar replaced with a freestanding wooden communion table.

The survival of the church is remarkable. There was a serious fire on Good Friday 1850 – hence the font by Philip Hardwick and the pulpit by his pupil Arthur Blomfield. It was Hardwick and John Morris who oversaw the sympathetic restoration. Further repair was needed after wartime bomb damage in 1940.

Yet more restoration was undertaken in the 1980s when Julian Harrap added tubular steel trusses to support the roof and the London Docklands Development Corporation cleaned the exterior. The churchyard with its unusual pyramid tomb and yellow crocuses in spring was landscaped. In 1803 the original churchyard was slightly reduced by the laying out of Commercial Road to link London with East India and West India Docks.

The church displays its Sir John Betjeman Award for repairs to the tower. But interior restoration of the walls above the galleries and the plaster ceiling continues slowly.

At first the parish was made up of people involved in river work. An 1853

St Anne's, Limehouse

memorial is to William Curling who is called 'an eminent shipbuilder of this parish'. Charles Dickens' godfather, Christopher Huffam, was a rigger who lived at 11 Newell Street on the corner of St Anne's Passage.

A plaque recalls John Birch who was rector from 1920 to 1955 and author of a history of Limehouse.

This is a lively church in the evangelical tradition, with a vicar, associate vicar and curate. On Sunday morning worshippers sit not in the pews but on red seats in a semicircle. A children's Sunday Club meets in the crypt during the service.

Open Monday to Friday 2pm to 4pm; weekends 2pm to 5.30pm
Commercial Road E14 7HP
www.stanneslimehouse.org

{ 23 }

12

St Anselm and St Cecilia, Kingsway

Roman Catholic

The church, with offices each side, opens directly on to Kingsway. The interior is small and simple.

It was built in 1909 and the architect, F. A. Walters, had to re-create the original church which had stood to the south in a street that ran under a house on the west side of Lincoln's Inn Fields.

This church dated from 1671 and was known as the Sardinian Chapel. It was in turn a successor to the secret Mass centre of penal times in The Ship Tavern in nearby Little Turnstile.

It was an embassy chapel and at first it suffered attacks. In 1688 the Franciscans in charge were driven out, but later it heard the first performances of many Mozart and Haydn Masses. Fanny Burney married General D'Arblay there. Until Westminster Cathedral opened, the old chapel hosted the annual Red Mass at the opening of the legal year.

The church remained under the patronage of the King of Sardinia until 1858. It had been dedicated to the eleventh-century Archbishop of Canterbury St Anselm, as he was born in Savoy and the House of Savoy ruled Sardinia. In 1861 the chapel took its present double dedication to St Anselm and St Cecilia. Ronald Knox preached about St Cecilia in the new church.

The move north was caused by slum clearance to make way for the new Kingsway. *The Tablet*, at the time of the dismantling, described the old church as having a 'prayer impregnated roof'.

The new church has a large painting after Corregio of the Deposition from the old chapel. The Sardinian royal arms are at the west end. Also brought here is the organ on which the organist Thomas Arne composed the tune for 'Rule Britannia'.

In the south aisle, added in 1954, is the Lady Chapel. The altar is from the old chapel and includes a stone from the Lady Chapel at Glastonbury Abbey. There is also a Chapel of St Thomas More who was a Bencher of Lincoln's Inn.

A tablet in the main church recalls Francis Bartlett who was parish priest from 1977 to 1985. He had been administrator of Westminster Cathedral where his brother was the last person to hold the office of Gentile Uomo, or Gentleman at Arms, to the cardinal.

St Anselm and St Cecilia, Kingsway

St Anselm's is the last of three great churches in Kingsway. Holy Trinity opposite, also rebuilt in 1909 and with a frontage based on Santa Maria della Pace in Rome, and Methodist Kingsway Hall, which drew large numbers to hear Donald Soper, have both closed.

The Guild of Our Lady of Ransom holds an annual Mass for the conversion of England and its annual walk to the Shrine of Our Lady at Walsingham sets out from here.

On Sunday there is a modern Latin Mass beautifully sung and attended by residents, hospital workers and visitors. Prayers often include mention of the sick children at nearby Great Ormond Street Hospital.

Open daily
Kingsway WC2A 3JA
www.rcdow.org.uk/lincolnsinnfields

13
The Assumption, Warwick Street
Roman Catholic

This building behind Regent Street appears from the road to be just a terrace of houses.

The church opened in 1730 as a chapel in converted stables for the Portuguese Embassy in Golden Square behind. After 1747, when the house became the Bavarian Embassy, the church was known as the Royal Bavarian Chapel. After being badly damaged in the 1780 Gordon Riots, the plain frontage was retained in the rebuilding.

Among worshippers in the 1790s, when diplomats sat in the gallery, was the Prince Regent's wife Maria Fitzherbert. At that time, this was one of the few churches where one could attend a High Mass. The assistance of opera singers led to Mass being described as a 'shilling opera' by Protestants. Among those who experienced this rare Continental worship was Henry Newman, the future cardinal, who as a boy was brought once by his father. The aristocracy sat in pews while poor visitors were assigned to an open space. But by the early twentieth century the Duke of Norfolk, a parishioner, often sat with inmates from the Poland Street workhouse.

John Francis Wade attended when he wrote the words and music of 'Adeste Fidelis' ('O come, all ye faithful') which was first known as the Portuguese hymn. The Irish politician Daniel O'Connell came to the church when in London. In 1861 Sir Richard Burton, the nineteenth-century explorer and translator of the *Kama Sutra*, was married here.

Prayers for the King of Bavaria continued to be said after Mass until 1871 when the country became part of Germany and the ambassador was withdrawn from London, leaving the chapel to become a parish church. It is generally known as 'the Warwick Street Church' but the official name is 'The Church of Our Lady of the Assumption and St Gregory'. The 'St' came first, with 'the Assumption' added in 1854. But the Bavarian coat of arms survives and the embassy has become the rectory and parish hall.

The church interior appears much as it did in the eighteenth century thanks to the failure of a rebuilding appeal a century later. The gallery gives the building the feel of a nonconformist church spoilt only by the 1875 reworking of the apse by John Francis Bentley. The Assumption relief by J. E. Carew, the focus above the altar for 20 years, has been moved to the side.

The Assumption, Warwick Street

An awkwardly placed side altar arrived in 1958 from the chapel of Foxcote House in Warwickshire which, like this church, was a Mass centre in penal times. Our Lady's statue is crowned with a diadem made in the parish by the Crown Jewellers.

In 1958 this was among the first churches to have a Sunday evening Mass due to a number of Irish catering workers arriving in Soho. More recently, the church has been the venue for Masses where gay people are made particularly welcome. On Sundays, printed translations of the readings are available in French, Italian, Spanish and, appropriately, German.

Open daily
Warwick Street WIF 9JR
www.rcdow.org.uk/warwickstreet

14

St Augustine's, Kilburn

Anglican

The 254-foot steeple rises above ugly flats to keep the red-brick St Augustine's as a landmark in a much changed streetscape and a guide to visitors arriving at Kilburn Park Station.

The church is a breakaway from St Mary's, Kilburn, where in 1867 the curate, Fr Richard Kirkpatrick, a friend of Dr Edward Pusey, found the new vicar too low church.

The curate and a number of lay people resigned and, with the permission of the Bishop of London, founded a mission district nearby. Within three years a swampy site was obtained for a new church. In 1871 both a temporary church opened and a foundation stone was laid.

Fr Kirkpatrick chose J. L. Pearson as the architect, having seen his recently completed St Peter's in Vauxhall. For Kilburn, Pearson took inspiration from Albi Cathedral in France, especially for the galleries, and Saint-Étienne at Caen. The result led to Pearson receiving the commission for Truro Cathedral. The astonishing thirteenth-century-style church was consecrated in 1880.

Beyond the five-arch rood screen is an outstanding stone chancel packed with statues. Giles Gilbert Scott added to Pearson's high altar reredos as well as providing the Lady Chapel reredos.

John Betjeman suggested walking round this galleried church watching the changing vista. In 1996 St Augustine's itself was considered impressive enough to double for St George's Chapel Windsor in the film *Mrs Brown*.

For many years the tower stood in an unfinished state but was finally crowned by the spire in 1898 when 75-year-old Fr Kirkpatrick was hoisted 240 feet up on a small platform in order to lay and bless the top stone.

An infamous parishioner was the anti-Ritualist campaigner John Kensit who in 1901 had managed to nominate himself as churchwarden. His lack of success at the parish meeting led to the calling of a parish poll where he was defeated by 290 votes to 49. At this time, Sunday attendance was around 600.

Still in use is a fine collection of vestments by J. D. and Edmund Sedding and G. E. Street. Some were made by the Sisters of the Church, an order founded in the parish before the church was opened and now found in four countries.

More than half of the now multiracial congregation lives locally. Children

St Augustine's, Kilburn

from the primary school come on special occasions. The magnificent church is sometimes the venue for national festivals such as the Additional Curates Society annual gathering. The building has been used for many recordings and in the 1970s BBC Promenade Concerts were broadcast live.

There is daily Mass. At the main Sunday Mass the procession enters along the north side, appearing and disappearing behind the pillars. Even after the re-ordering, a shaft of sunlight can still sometimes fall on the facing altar as incense hangs briefly like a cobweb in the light above. There is evensong and Benediction in the evening.

Open Saturday 10am to noon
Kilburn Park Road NW6 5XB
www.saint-augustine.org.uk

15

St Barnabas, Pimlico

Anglican

A pristine stone spire rises above a large ragstone church which looks bigger than it is due to an integrated school and clergy house. The church interior is small but full of treasures and decoration.

This, the first purpose-built Anglo-Catholic church, was founded by St Paul's in Knightsbridge, after its vicar, William Bennett, had called on its wealthy congregation to care for the poor at the Pimlico end of the large parish.

'Come with me and visit the dens of infamy, and the haunts of vice, ignorance, filth and atheism with which it abounds,' appealed Father Bennett. 'Then look at your noble houses, the gold that glitters on your sideboard, and the jewels that gleam on your bosoms, and say within your secret conscience, as standing before the great and terrible God at the day of Judgement, "What shall I do, if I give not of the one to relieve the other?"'

St Barnabas, opened in 1851, was described as 'the most sumptuous and correctly fitted church erected in England since the Reformation'. Later there would be a rood screen by Bodley and a Lady Chapel by Comper who was married here. The Bishop of London was not happy and *Punch* attacked the catholic practices. William Bennett was forced to resign after a year and moved to Somerset where in 1854 he invented the parish magazine.

The criticism frightened away curate Frederick Ouseley, who had used his fortune to fund the organ and start a choir. But good music continued with priest-organist George Herbert Palmer who was succeeded by composer Basil Harwood, now buried in the chancel and known for the tune 'Almondsbury'.

In 1894 curate George Woodward became precentor and encouraged plainsong and medieval music. Before leaving in 1899 he published *Hymns and Carols for Christmas-tide*. At the start of the twentieth century, when Vaughan Williams was organist, the compilers of the first *English Hymnal* often met here.

John Keble, J. M. Neale, Dr Edward Pusey and Henry Manning all preached from the pulpit. Charles Lowder was a curate when he founded the Society of St John of the Cross (SSJ) for catholic Anglican clergy.

In 1888 priest-in-charge Alfred Gurney became Aubrey Beardsley's first patron by commissioning a Christmas card. After High Mass, 16-year-old Beardsley and his mother sometimes lunched in the clergy house where the young artist gazed at the

St Barnabas, Pimlico

Pre-Raphaelite pictures. Other guests might include Lord Halifax, and sometimes the well-read and well-connected Fr Gurney would recall his conversations with Dante Gabriel Rossetti or discuss the latest opera.

A World War Two curate was the Mirfield monk Harry Williams who in 1981 led prayers at Prince Charles' wedding.

Towards the end of the twentieth century the working-class residents had largely drained away and attendance dwindled. Since 2006 the new landmark spire has brought rebirth as it draws into the church passengers killing time at Victoria Coach Station.

Open Wednesday, Friday and Saturday 12am to 3pm
St Barnabas Street SW1W 8PF
www.stbarnabaspimlico.org.uk

16
St Bartholomew the Great, Smithfield
Anglican

This church is hidden beyond a partly thirteenth-century timber-framed archway in Smithfield. The building is only revealed to passers-by in narrow Cloth Fair which runs behind the meat market's main through road. Here a blue plaque indicates that one of the houses was the home of Sir John Betjeman.

Inside the church there is collegiate seating and Norman arches beyond the altar. A dark ambulatory leads the visitor to a light Lady Chapel which since 1998 has been dominated by a striking painting of the Virgin and Child by Spanish painter Alfredo Roldan. The same space was in 1725 a temporary print shop employing Benjamin Franklin as the apprentice.

The church is the remains of a monastery built on open land outside the City in 1123 as a thanksgiving for recovery from illness. Rahere, whose body now lies in this church, was nursed in Rome at the hospital attached to St Bartholomew on Tiber Island. London's St Bart's Hospital was founded as part of Rahere's Augustinian priory.

Today's church is just the east end of the great priory church. Inserted into the Norman arcading above the choir is an extraordinary oriel window giving a view down on to the founder's tomb. Also surviving is a portion of cloister restored in the 1890s by the churchwarden's brother Sir Aston Webb, and now a cafe. Artist William Hogarth was baptized at the medieval font.

The building has featured in numerous films including *Shakespeare in Love*, *The End of the Affair*, *Amazing Grace* and *The Other Boleyn Girl*. It is the fifth church featured in *Four Weddings and a Funeral*.

The church's current statue of St Bartholomew is by Damien Hirst.

A noted twentieth-century rector was Newall Wallbank who was appointed curate in 1937, served as rector from 1945 to 1979, and died in this church during evensong in 1996. As curate he had responsibility from the start since the then rector, his godfather, usually set off for his home in Eastbourne during Sunday evensong, leaving young Wallbank to conclude the service.

On Good Friday the rector stands on a tombstone in the graveyard, once covered by the nave, to preside at a distribution of hot cross buns. This is just part of the

St Bartholomew the Great, Smithfield

Butterworth Charity which also provides 6d for any parish widow. For a few years after decimalization the rector put an old sixpence in his cassock pocket on Good Friday but it was never claimed.

The bells, installed in 1510 and heard by the Carthusian martyrs at nearby Charterhouse, ring out the oldest peal in the country. This is of course a popular church for weddings. The congregation enjoys a high standard of music and liturgy with processions at Epiphany, Palm Sunday and Corpus Christi.

This was the first church to have its web address on a banner, the first to have the euro symbol on its donation box, and the first London parish church to levy an admission charge.

Open daily; admission £4 (conc £3)
Smithfield EC1A 7JQ
www.greatstbarts.com

17

St Bartholomew the Less, Smithfield

Anglican

The octagonal church is hidden behind the gateway to St Bart's Hospital and is easily missed. Much rebuilding over the years means that, on entering, the visitor must leave the original stone floor and climb several steps to the main church which, given its confined location, is remarkably light.

The gateway, built in 1702 with stones left over from St Paul's Cathedral, includes London's only Henry VIII statue. He closed St Bartholomew's Priory in 1536 but saved its hospital. In 1547 he ordered the Chapel of the Holy Cross dating from 1123, one of the hospital's five chapels, to be retained and turned into a parish church with a parish boundary embracing just the hospital.

So the Holy Cross Chapel became St Bartholomew the Less to distinguish it from the priory church also turned into a parish church. The hospital church tower is fifteenth century and has bells dated 1400 and 1430.

George Dance the Younger, who was the hospital surveyor, designed a wooden octagon which was installed between 1789 and 1791 within existing and partly pre-Reformation walls. This wooden arrangement was renewed in stone in the 1820s by successor surveyor Thomas Hardwick, who built the hospital screen fronting Smithfield.

The main lasting effect of World War Two damage, which closed the church for a few years, was damage to the windows. The replacement glass at the east end by Hugh Easton was installed in 1951 and features St Luke, patron of doctors, and St Bartholomew with his arm round the hospital founder, Rahere. A war memorial window shows a kneeling nurse.

There are numerous plaques to medical staff. Queen Elizabeth I's doctor, sergeant surgeon Robert Balthorpe, is commemorated on the south wall. In the vestry there is a sixteenth-century tomb of Elizabeth Freke and her surgeon husband John.

One memorial is to Anne Bodley who is buried here. Her husband, Bodleian Library founder Sir Thomas Bodley, wrote the inscription recording their happy marriage. They lived at the hospital in later years and Sir Thomas also died here although his body was taken to Oxford and buried in Merton College chapel.

Architect Inigo Jones, son of a Smithfield clothworker, was baptized here in 1573. Thomas Monro, a member of a well-known medical family, was vicar and hospitaller from 1754 to 1765.

St Bartholomew the Less, Smithfield

The gatehouse and church exterior are attractive enough to feature briefly as an inn of court in the second Bridget Jones film, *The Edge of Reason*.

Being a parish church, this is a hospital chapel in the unique position of having not only a vicar and hospitaller instead of a chaplain but also churchwardens and a parochial church council. Anglican and Roman Catholic Masses are celebrated on Sunday and alternately on weekday lunchtimes. Many call in to pray for sick friends and relatives. The small warmly carpeted church with gothic pews is also a venue for medical family weddings, christenings and memorial services.

Open daily
Smithfield EC1A 7BE
www.bartsandthelondon.nhs.uk

18
Bloomsbury Baptist Church
Baptist

A surprise among the trees at the north end of Shaftesbury Avenue is what appears to be a large French church with a rose window. Inside the illusion is dashed by a semicircle which could double as a council chamber.

The church's full but little-used title is Bloomsbury Central Baptist Church, but usually the 'Central' is dropped. It was built in 1848 by Sir Morton Peto MP, a former Anglican and a railway contractor, who decided on a fine building after the Crown Commissioners, who were the landlords, appeared reluctant to permit a nonconformist church in case it was ugly.

Peto is said to have exclaimed: 'A spire, My Lord? We shall have two.' There are two Romanesque towers, although their spires have now been removed having been declared unsafe after a century. The Caen stone on the frontage had to be replaced with Portland stone as early as 1876. But it is still an attractive building.

Its first minister was William Brock who used the Bible and *The Times* as his guide for preaching. In 1851, anticipating overseas visitors coming to London for the Great Exhibition, Brock ruled that Americans practising or condoning slavery would not be welcome at the Lord's table.

It became the Baptists' Central Church in 1905, which saved the church from possible closure as the lease was running out and many members of the congregation were moving to the suburbs. However, with the freehold purchased, the mission continued to be to Bloomsbury. A later minister was Dr F. Townley Lord who also edited the *Baptist Times* and served as President of the Baptist World Alliance in the 1950s.

When Dr Howard Williams became minister in the 1960s a reconstruction programme saw the re-ordering of the church and the upper gallery removed. The rose window was revealed from the inside for the very first time. There is now an unusual baptismal pool in front of the pulpit. A side chapel created in 1999 has a mural with scenes of West End life in the 1960s painted as a reminder that the church is set in a city to share in its life. The building is much used by charities for meetings and by production companies for auditions and rehearsals.

Unusually for a Baptist church it has continued, as in 1851, to make strong public stands by being one of the first to become a Fair Trade church and opposing the war in Iraq. The mission statement claims that 'in faith and with openness to

Bloomsbury Baptist Church

different points of view, we search together for a better understanding of life and a deeper awareness of God'.

The continued drift of residents out of central London means that the Sunday congregation is made up of mainly a small group of local people supplemented by visitors from thriving provincial and American Baptist churches.

The Friendship Centre is open after morning service when homeless people join the congregation for traditional Sunday lunch.

Open daily
Shaftesbury Avenue WC2H 8EP
www.bloomsbury.org.uk

St Botolph-without-Bishopsgate
Anglican

The church stands at the approach to Liverpool Street Station but, as the name indicates, it was at first outside the city wall.

The outline of a Saxon church has been discovered on the site. An Elizabethan church survived the Great Fire but this was demolished in 1724 to make way for the fourth and present church.

Architects James Gould and his son-in-law George Dance the Elder placed the tower at the east end next to the street which meant that the public had to enter the church on either side of the altar. In 1892 today's main entrance in the churchyard was created by John Francis Bentley.

This enables the visitor to immediately stand at the west end and appreciate the long building lit by a 1828 dome lantern above the nave. Along the edge of the gallery are the names of incumbents from 1323. Alfred Earle was both rector and Bishop of Marlborough in the 1890s. Four of his successors were also simultaneously Bishops of Kensington or Willesden, including Gerald Ellison who became Bishop of London.

Alan Tanner was rector in 1993 when the church was damaged by an IRA bomb outside. Afterwards he and his congregation wore hard hats during the Eucharist rather than close the church until restoration was completed four years later.

William Rogers, rector from 1863 to 1896, founded the nearby Bishopsgate Institute. He was also associated with the rebuilding of Dulwich College whose founder, Edward Alleyn, had been baptized in the ancient church.

Brought to the present building as babies for christening were the first feminist writer Mary Wollstonecraft in 1759, and poet John Keats in 1795. Buried here are Ben Jonson's infant son, and Sir Paul Pindar whose Bishopsgate house is preserved in the Victoria & Albert Museum.

The Honourable Artillery Company's chapel is on the north side. A recent addition near the back of the church is a memorial to those who have died from HIV or hepatitis as a result of contaminated blood. They are also remembered at an annual commemoration.

The Bowyers' Company, who hold an annual service, commissioned the modern window featuring bows by Nicola Kantorowicz to mark the post-bombing restoration.

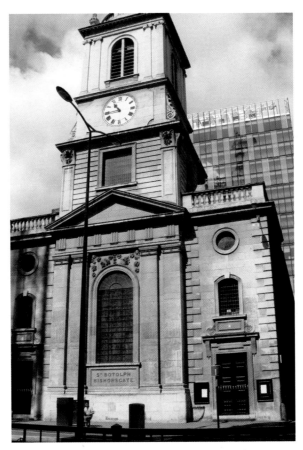

St Botolph-without-Bishopsgate

The bells are rung every Wednesday lunchtime for a Sung Eucharist. The mission here is to commuters working in City offices on weekdays, so on Sundays the church is lent to members of the Antochian Orthodox Church who commute in from the suburbs.

The churchyard was the first to become a City Corporation garden and includes a tennis court as well as the tomb of Eagle Star co-founder Sir William Rawlins. There is also the oldest Great War memorial, dating from 1916. The church hall is a former school, with nineteenth-century figures of a boy and girl flanking the doorway. More extraordinary is the replica of Christ's tomb which was erected in 1894 as the entrance to a Turkish bath.

Open Monday to Friday 9am to 5.30pm
Bishopsgate EC2M 3TL
www.botolph.org.uk

St Bride's, Fleet Street

Anglican

Known as the journalists' church, the spire of St Bride's can be seen from Fleet Street – but only through a gap created in 1824 when number 84, a bookshop, was burnt down.

The nave pews are built in the collegiate style with each seat sponsored by a newspaper or dedicated to a journalist. One carries the name of Edgar Wallace who sold newspapers at Ludgate Circus before becoming an editor and novelist. Below is a crypt with traces of Roman work.

On this site, the Normans rebuilt an existing church dedicated to St Bridget who has now become St Bride. Christopher Wren's replacement church following the Great Fire was his most expensive. His steeple, the model for the traditional wedding cake first made by a Ludgate Hill baker, was added in 1703. The church, hit by a World War Two bomb in 1940, has been rebuilt within its Wren walls.

A new plaque, unveiled by Simon Jenkins, recalls Caxton's apprentice Wynkyn de Worde who started the association with print when he set up his printing press next door. His woodcuts are occasionally used on service sheets. Diarist Samuel Pepys, who with his eight brothers and sisters was baptized here, records bribing the gravedigger in 1664 with sixpence to 'justle together' bodies in the crypt and make room for his brother Tom.

Within the parish in 1702, as its Wren church was almost complete, London's first daily newspaper, the *Daily Courant*, was born.

After the twentieth-century war damage the nave was rededicated in 1957 in the presence of the Queen and Prince Philip who returned for the 50th anniversary. 'The journalists and printers may have departed Fleet Street, but it is good to know that

St Bride's, Fleet Street

St Bride's, interior

St Bride's remains,' commented the *Evening Standard* in 2007. Sam White spent years in Paris as correspondent for the paper but his funeral was at St Bride's.

When the *Daily Express* axed the William Hickey diary it was at the St Bride's doorway that *Daily Mail* rival Nigel Dempster staged a mock funeral. His own memorial service was also held here.

John McCarthy, after being held hostage in Lebanon, came to the altar where prayers had been offered for him. BBC reporter Alan Johnson who was held hostage in Gaza said: 'This church stood by me in my darkest hour.'

Agricultural journalists organize the harvest festival which is followed by an auction of fruit, vegetables and honey. There is also a harvest of printing, when over 300 newspaper front pages are exhibited. St Bride's has maintained a focus for journalists despite the slow departure from Fleet Street which began in 1986 and was completed in 2005 when Reuters left its Lutyens building alongside the churchyard.

Services are enhanced by a professional choir. The Vigil on Easter morning, which begins in darkness with the fire being lit beneath the tower and ends with egg rolling down Fleet Street, always attracts a large congregation.

Open daily
Fleet Street EC4Y 8AU
www.stbrides.com

Christ Church, Blackfriars Road

Anglican

Christ Church is an ugly 1959 brick church created by architects R. Paxton Watson and B. Costin, who had a free hand thanks to wartime bombing which badly damaged the seventeenth-century building.

The church is the third on the site that is the centre of Paris Garden, mentioned by Shakespeare in *Henry VIII*. The parish boundary remains that of the ancient garden with a loop added to embrace Tate Modern. The first church was built in 1671, some 40 years after the death of John Marshall whose will provided for a church in Paris Garden. He had lived through the Gunpowder Plot and had become so anti-Catholic that he believed that Anglican churches should be built in the new suburbs.

Unfortunately this first church slowly sank into the boggy ground. The rebuild was undertaken between 1738 and 1741 and included a tower that became a landmark in the fields below St Paul's on the hill across the Thames. Southwark-born artist Thomas Girtin depicted the church from the river.

The first surprise inside is the huge picture of Wall Street's cityscape behind the altar. It is scenery rescued from the nearby National Theatre. Also intriguing is the stained glass. Nave windows depict baking and printing, which were major local industries, a bus and Tate Modern as a power station. A window added in 1984 shows a supermarket trolley to recall Sainsbury's headquarters alongside the churchyard.

The postwar church was first a focus for the ecumenical South London Industrial Mission with ten chaplains serving factories and offices. Also here was the pioneering Southwark Ordination Course.

Today the rooms are home to several organizations including the SE1 community website, Sesame Institute and the South Bank Alexander Centre. The Confraternity of Saint James, promoting the pilgrim route to Santiago de Compostela, receives would-be pilgrims preparing for their walk of a lifetime.

The John Marshall Hall within the complex is used for yoga, Blackfriars Sinfonia rehearsals, union meetings and conferences. It is a deliberate policy to make the church visibly engage with society. On the hall's wall is Ian Walters' *New Regime* sculpture, depicting the traumatic forced move from Fleet Street faced by print workers whose crisis meetings were held in the space.

Christ Church, Blackfriars Road

The church is rare in being owned and maintained by a trust rather than the Southwark Diocese. The churchyard, cared for by the Bankside Open Spaces Trust, is unusual in having the Rose & Crown in one corner where hops cascade from archways.

This is a centre of worship and community involvement. It is also a church at the heart of regeneration, and planned high-rise buildings on all four sides will leave Christ Church as dwarfed as the church in Wall Street. Appropriately, the rector is the Bishop's Adviser on Regeneration.

On Sunday it is so quiet that even the pub is closed but there are enough local residents to maintain a parish communion.

Open Monday to Friday 8.30am to lunchtime
Blackfriars Road SE1 8NY
www.christchurchsouthwark.org.uk

22

Christ Church, Spitalfields

Anglican

The 225-foot-high stone tower rising above four Tuscan columns is the focus of Brushfield Street, and H. S. Goodhart-Rendel considered this English baroque building to be probably the finest church in Europe.

Spitalfields recalls the Priory of St Mary Spital which stood on the site of Old Spitalfields Market from 1197 to 1538. Within 200 years the growing population, many French Protestants, resulted in the building of this new church designed by Nicholas Hawksmoor. Work started in 1714 and continued until 1729.

The church was closed for safety in 1958 and a Friends of Christ Church was formed to stop demolition. Generous support from the National Lottery helped the £10 million restoration which took longer than the original construction.

It allowed for unsuitable Victorian additions to be removed, and now the interior that was re-opened in 2004 looks as it did in about 1750, but without the box pews. Lost galleries have been rebuilt and the walls painted white. The east end has a Venetian window and a chancel entered beneath a high classical rood bearing the weight of the royal arms.

On each side there are large monuments. One is a bust of Edward Peck who laid the foundation stone. The memorial is by mason Thomas Dunn who built the church. Opposite is Flaxman's figure of Sir Robert Ladbroke dressed as Lord Mayor of London. His wife Elizabeth, was Peck's granddaughter.

A 2005 memorial honours architect James Stirling who knew and admired the church and its architect all his adult life.

The organ, when installed by Richard Bridge in 1735, was the largest in England with 2,000 pipes and continued to hold the record until the next century. Handel is believed to have played it. After 1960 it ceased to be used until it was rescued by art dealer and organ expert Michael Gillingham, who lived in a Georgian house behind the church.

The crypt has been cleared of 1,000 bodies to enable a new use and now morning prayer is said there.

When Henry Smith, founder of WH Smith, was married in 1784 his bride signed the register with an X. John Wesley, whose mother was born in Spitalfields, preached here. Curate Samuel Henshall invented the Henshall corkscrew patented in 1795 for 'extracting the hardest, tightest or most decayed cork'.

Christ Church, Spitalfields

The use of chairs for seating allows the repaved Purbeck stone nave to be a flexible space available for dinners and even the Spitalfields Ball. Art displayed has included work by local artists Gilbert & George.

There is a Sunday service and a mission of 'growing the church and blessing the community' involving many outreach activities, although the restored Christ Church is too minimalist to have kneelers for prayers. Instead it is best known for its magnificent acoustic with concerts not only at lunchtime but during both the summer and winter Spitalfields Festivals once directed by Richard Hickox. The Friends who saved this church remain a driving force to maintain the fabric.

Open Monday to Friday 11am to 4pm; Sundays 1pm to 4pm
Commercial Street E1 6QE
www.ccspitalfields.org

23
Christ the King, Bloomsbury
Anglican

Christ the King looks like a foreign cathedral and only the red phone boxes under the fig trees confirm that this is London and not Paris. But it is the even more impressive interior that is much praised.

The church, built of Bath stone in 1850–4 for a new sect called the Catholic Apostolic Church, was designed by gothic expert Raphael Brandon. In 1963, after the death of the last Catholic Apostolic priest, it became the University of London's Anglican chapel. The first Church of England service was an early morning Eucharist celebrated by the Bishop of London, Robert Stopford.

At once Sir John Betjeman wrote to the chaplaincy: 'I am so glad that you are being allowed to use the Catholic Apostolic Church in Gordon Square as a chapel for London University. Good heavens! You couldn't have a grander chapel. Why, even the nave of Westminster Abbey is only thirteen feet higher than the nave and sanctuary of Gordon Square. You have not got just a chapel for London University, but a cathedral.'

He enthusiastically stressed that it was a building for worship, not for lectures: 'Notice how the hammerbeam roof with its rich carving soars almost out of sight, becomes a stone vaulted roof over the sanctuary, and then leads the eye down the long-drawn vista to the pinnacled tabernacle . . .'

Unlike in earlier times, the services were crowded during these student years. The best attended were always on Ash Wednesday and Ascension Day when often the Archbishop of Canterbury was present. Whether it was term time or vacation, Holy Week was faithfully observed and climaxed with a then rare dawn Easter Vigil.

In 1983 Sir Nikolaus Pevsner's memorial service was held here in the church which he had described in *The Buildings of England* as being 'on a cathedral scale and in a cathedral style'.

The chaplains during these years of growth included Michael Marshall, later Bishop of Woolwich; Peter Delaney, who became Archdeacon of London; and future Dean of Guildford Victor Stock. The director of music was the versatile Professor Ian Hall.

Visiting preachers included Cardinal Giovanni Benelli of Florence who came days before a conclave where he was a favourite for the papal throne.

Christ the King, Bloomsbury

The University abandoned the church suddenly in July 1992 for mainly financial reasons. The great building is now the 'cathedral' for Forward in Faith, the Anglican group that looks to flying bishops for protection from women's priestly ministry. There is no Sunday service.

Only the English Chapel, where the congregation sits in arcading on each side, is open daily but from the altar it is possible to look west down the soaring nave. The cloisters are also closed but once a month there is a lunchtime organ recital when visitors can enjoy the main church.

Open Monday to Friday 8am to 4pm
Gordon Square WC1H 0AG
www.forwardinfaith.com

24

St Clement Danes, Strand

Anglican

This is one of the two churches in the The Strand with traffic flowing on two sides. It has a pristine interior. Samuel Johnson, who regularly sat in the gallery near the pulpit, has a statue outside the east end which has become a gathering point for television journalists reporting from the Royal Courts of Justice opposite.

The name suggests that Danish traders once lived here at Aldwych and the link was renewed in the 1920s when Danes attended services. Although the church escaped the Great Fire it was rebuilt in 1681 by Christopher Wren. The steeple was added to the tower in 1719 by James Gibbs while working on nearby St Mary-le-Strand. Wren had retained a recently built tower resulting in his church remaining on the same alignment as the old – which is not east–west but at a more awkward angle to the road than St Mary-le-Strand.

Before World War Two this was called both the Church of Flower Sellers and the Australian Church since Australia Day in January and ANZAC Day in April were observed, with services attended by staff from Australia House opposite.

In 1941 St Clement's was gutted by a German incendiary bomb and over the next decade weeds and bushes grew within the shelter of the walls. In 1958 it re-opened, having been restored as the Central Church of the Royal Air Force and a living memorial to those who died while serving in the RAF. Outside the west door, the statue of William Gladstone has been joined by those of Air Chief Marshall Lord Dowding and Sir Arthur 'Bomber' Harris.

Books of remembrance record the names of over 155,000 men and women who died on active service and set in the wide aisle floor are 750 RAF badges. The font is in the crypt where poet John Donne's wife Ann was among the burials. This is one of the few places where one can see gold, frankincense and myrrh. This example of the Magi's gifts was presented in 1971 by the RAF Station at Muharraq in Bahrain to mark its closure.

In 1676 Sir Thomas Grosvenor married heiress Mary Davies, enabling him to found the Grosvenor Estate. Around 25 service personnel are married here each year.

Those killed in conflict today are remembered shortly after their death during a celebration of the Eucharist when family members are often present. There is also an annual service in November for those who have died in the past year.

St Clement Danes and statue of Samuel Johnson, Strand

The Oranges and Lemons nursery rhyme is rung on a carillon four times a day although the song may refer to St Clement Eastcheap. Every spring, in a tradition dating only from 1920, children from St Clement Danes School in Drury Lane attend an Oranges and Lemons Service. On leaving the west door each child is given an orange and a lemon.

Open daily 9am to 4pm
Strand WC2R 1DH
www.raf.mod.uk/stclementdanes

25

Corpus Christi, Maiden Lane

Roman Catholic

This easily missed church has a brick frontage built flush with the pavement in Covent Garden's narrow Maiden Lane. As building work began in 1873, Rules restaurant across the road was celebrating its 75th anniversary and it is only from this distance that the existence of the church is apparent.

To enter the church you must go down steps into a covered entrance and lean on a door on the right. The interior is like a grotto with little natural light. Although hidden, there is a constant trickle of people dropping in to pray.

The architect was Frederick H. Pownall, an Anglo-Catholic living in Gower Street and who, a decade earlier, had designed St Peter's, London Docks. His son became rector of The Assumption, Warwick Street. The font, which may be fifteenth century, was unearthed during the deep excavation needed in the confined site. The latest addition is an appropriate statue of St Tarsicius by Karin Jonzen installed in 1998. This third-century saint, who at first appears to be looking at his mobile, is hiding the Host from a pagan mob that is about to kill him.

When opened, this was only the second church to have the Corpus Christi dedication. The first was the pre-Reformation St Mary & Corpus Christi at Down Hatherley in Gloucestershire. The dedication is reflected in the east windows above the altar which show Juliana of Liege, who founded the festival in 1246, and St Thomas Aquinas who scripted the liturgy. They were given in 1876 by Percy Fitzgerald, a friend of Charles Dickens. Four years later the new rector was Francis Stanfield who wrote the popular Corpus Christi hymn 'Sweet sacrament divine'. Until 1974, when Covent Garden Market moved away, the little church was always decorated with plenty of flowers on the feast day.

Poet Francis Thompson was a frequent worshipper, and in the early twentieth century Ronald Knox preached here on at least 26 occasions.

This much loved church attracts good numbers and sometimes there are children's Masses attended by pupils from the nearby school. Based here is the Catholic Stage Guild – handily close to St Paul's, the Anglican Actors' Church. The statue of the Guild's patron, St Genesius, is near the Lady Chapel. But for major services there is an even stronger second congregation made up of Latin Mass Society members which means that on Holy Saturday, for example, the Easter

Corpus Christi, Maiden Lane

Vigil is celebrated twice, first in Latin with the Tridentine rite and then at the normal time in English.

Open daily
Maiden Lane WC2E 7NB
www.maidenlane.org.uk

26

St Cuthbert's, Philbeach Gardens
Anglican

This church is familiar to railway passengers who catch its dark brick east end on high ground from the West London line. In Philbeach Gardens this brick building stands out against white stucco houses.

The lofty church with a crypt was built between 1884 and 1888, starting with a foundation stone brought from Holy Island. The architect was Hugh Roumieu Gough.

The inside is much more exciting having been much embellished over subsequent years. This additional decoration and furnishing started immediately under the church's founder and first vicar Henry Westall, who cemented the very strong Anglo-Catholic tradition.

He was handed a gothic church with marble piers and walls. The very substantial rood screen, like a Tower Bridge walkway, was added in 1893. Six years later Fr Ernest Geldart designed a huge reredos which was eventually installed just before World War One. It can only be rivalled by one in a Spanish church or at New York's St Thomas Church Fifth Avenue.

The furnishings are Arts and Crafts, with a hint of Art Nouveau, thanks to William Bainbridge Reynolds who was an early member of the congregation. He hand-made the extraordinary iron and copper lectern. He was also responsible for the communion rails, paschal candlestick, screens and a representation of the royal arms looking as if it had been purchased at Liberty's.

Stone panelling was added where there was no marble. The large stations of the cross painted by Franz Vinck hang like old masters down each side of the church.

During the early years the church enjoyed a Sunday congregation of around 450 who strongly supported its much criticized ritualism. The miserichords include the head with asses' ears of John Kensit, the Protestant agitator, who invaded the church with his supporters on Good Friday 1898. The giant pulpit has miniatures of Anglo-Catholic pioneers Thomas Carter, Edward King, Edward Pusey and John Keble.

At one time the church was open for prayer from 6.30am to 9.30pm. Today, although not open all hours, the still firmly catholic St Cuthbert's seeks to be a centre of prayer in busy Earls Court where the dominant building is not now the church but the giant exhibition hall.

St Cuthbert's, Philbeach Gardens

The adjoining 1894 Philbeach Hall provides weekday support to those who could become marginalized in the teeming area.

Around 25 different languages are spoken in the church's primary school by children whose families come from many countries. The pupils come to St Cuthbert's for such occasions as harvest festival and some sing or play an instrument at the carol service.

This is a valued venue for the Earls Court Festival. The Earls Court Baroque, a period-instrument ensemble dedicated to the exploration of repertoire from the Baroque era, gives regular concerts.

But the big occasion that draws vi itors from outside the parish is St Cuthbert's Day – 20 March – when three relics of the saint are brought out.

Open Sunday mornings 9am to 1pm
Philbeach Gardens sw5 9eb
www.saintcuthbert.org

27

St Cyprian's, Clarence Gate

Anglican

This church in Glentworth Street is brick and easily missed as it appears to merge with a high brick mansion block. Architectural writer Anthony Symondson has described the interior as 'a fusion of controlled austerity and splendour'.

The rare dedication to St Cyprian, Bishop of Carthage martyred in 258, was the choice of Fr Charles Gutch who died before the church was built. He ran a mission at the opposite end of the street from 1864 until his death in 1896. The landlord, the first Viscount Portman, had been reluctant to give land for a permanent building as he did not care for Fr Gutch's Tractarian views. But soon after his death the land was made available by the second Viscount, a former Liberal MP, as part of the street's redevelopment and work on a permanent church began in 1901.

The space was not ideal and the church had to be aligned north–south rather than east–west by the architect Sir Ninian Comper. He was preferred over G. E. Street by Lord Portman who did not want a French gothic building. Comper provided him with a Norfolk Perpendicular interior.

At the consecration in 1903 the floor was strewn with rushes and flowers as might have happened in medieval times. The inside is astonishingly light considering the exceptionally dark street. There is white glass in the nave, looking at night like stacks of empty wine bottles, and a generous stained glass window behind the altar.

But the overwhelming feature is the delicate rood screen running across the entire church, with saints depicted in panels along the bottom. There are no pews, and instead sparse rows of chairs allow for the nave to be utilized for liturgy. The altar has riddle-posts and for the first 30 years, in keeping with the furnishing, a form of the Sarum Rite was used at Mass.

In the 'north' chapel beyond the screen, where the altar is from the old church, the statue of St Cyprian is turned to gaze down the wide church with its painted roof. Comper was young enough when appointed to be able to continue the restrained decoration for over 50 years. Writer Ian Nairn considered this to be the most joyful church interior in London and enthused about light and space bouncing from wall to wall.

Poet T. S. Eliot, writer C. S. Lewis and pianist Geoffrey Parsons worshipped

St Cyprian's, Clarence Gate

here. P. D. James mentions the church in her novels. Organists include William Lloyd Webber.

The parish comprises just the few streets between Baker Street and Marylebone Stations. The congregation is small but St Cyprian's Day on 16 September attracts many visitors. Other annual occasions include the Advent Carol Service when the church is candlelit. Francis Holland School, founded by Canon Francis Holland, is across the road and the girls come for concerts and school services. The church is a popular venue for recitals and recordings.

Open on Thursday 11am to 2pm
Glentworth Street NW1 6AX
www.stcyprians.org.uk

28

St Dominic's, Haverstock Hill

Roman Catholic

The building is very large for a Roman Catholic church. The name is misleading for the landmark is not on the Haverstock Hill main road but just east in Southampton Road and almost adjoining the St Pancras Almshouses.

The homes were built in the 1850s just before the Dominican priory opened on adjacent land chosen by Cardinal Nicholas Wiseman. But work on the church itself did not begin until 1878 when the architect, whose three brothers were Dominicans, was Charles Buckler.

Inside, the exceptionally long nave is dominated by columns holding up the high roof. At first the church interior appears to be stone for the yellow brick merges well with the stone pillars and dressings. The full dedication is Our Lady of the Rosary and St Dominic which is explained by the 14 side chapels each dedicated to a mystery of the rosary.

In one chapel there is a Madonna shrine framed by a wooden canopy designed by Blore for Peterborough Cathedral. Another chapel became the Lourdes Chapel when a small replica of the shrine was erected there in 1914. Its recent £25,000 restoration paid for by jumble sales has proved a success and the chapel again attracts many visitors.

A surprise north transept with a freestanding vaulting shaft gives the building the feel of a cathedral. Here there is the recently restored Lady Chapel with its mosaics by the Salviati workshop in Venice. At the back of the church there is a column rescued from the site of Blackfriars Priory, the more famous Dominican house in the City of London.

Today some of the priory buildings have been sold but on the church's south side there is a garden sheltered by both the church and the main priory residence. The latter was designed by Gilbert Blount whose church plans were never realized. This is also the home of the Provincial of the Dominican friars in England and Scotland. Other residents have included Fr Vincent McNabb who in the 1930s regularly debated at Speakers' Corner. In 2009 the large church was crowded for the funeral of Fr Columba Ryan who days earlier had preached at the funeral of his brother, Pugwash cartoonist John Ryan.

There is a monthly Friday organ recital by guest organists playing the 1883 Henry Willis organ which 'Father' Willis himself thought was one of his best.

St Dominic's, Haverstock Hill

In the Lady Chapel there is an 1859 Henry Bryceson organ which the church's organist Martin Stacey recently rescued from neglect in Somerset.

Treasures include a chalice that belonged to Cardinal Philip Howard, the Dominican who negotiated the marriage of Charles II to Catherine of Braganza and helped to restore the English Dominican Province.

On Sundays, around 900 people join the friars for one of the four Masses. Children abound at the morning Mass while there is a quieter congregation for a midday Solemn Mass with a choir singing Latin parts.

Open daily
Southampton Road NW5 4LB
www.op-london.org

29

St Dunstan-in-the-West

Anglican

The lantern of St Dunstan's is framed by the Fleet Street buildings for those walking west thanks to a slight bend in the road. Halfway up the street the tower is then framed by the Royal Courts of Justice.

Outside there is a clock with two giants who strike the hours and a statue of Elizabeth I which once stood on the Lud Gate outside St Martin, Ludgate Hill. The entrance is directly off the pavement and leads to an interior which is in the form of an octagon.

The first mention of a church on this site is 1185. During the Great Fire of 1666 the Dean of Westminster roused the Abbey schoolboys in the middle of the night to bring buckets and defend ancient St Dunstan's, where the flames just missed the church.

But the widening of Fleet Street in 1829 caused the church's demolition and the present building was erected on the churchyard behind. The new church's dramatic lantern tower was inspired by All Saints Pavement in York where the tower was lit at night to guide travellers in the nearby countryside.

Bible translator William Tyndale was a curate here and shortly after poet John Donne was rector. Praisegod Barebones, who gave his name to Cromwell's Barebones Parliament, was married here, and Lord Baltimore, who gave his name to Baltimore in the USA, was buried in the old church. Angler Izaak Walton was a sidesman, and diarist Samuel Johnson found pretty women a distraction during the sermon. The Hoare family, whose bank has been opposite since 1690, has supplied churchwardens over the centuries.

The probably fictional eighteenth-century villain Sweeney Todd had the back door to his barber's shop in nearby Hen & Chickens Court. It has been claimed that those parts of the bodies that did not go into pies were placed in the crypt of the old church.

Although St Bride's at the opposite end of Fleet Street is the journalists' church, this one also has newspaper associations. Press baron Lord Rothermere brought back the clock, made for the first church, in 1936. Commemorated outside with an obelisk by Lutyens and a bust is his brother Lord Northcliffe who founded the *Daily Mail*. There is also a plaque to J. L. Garvin who edited the *Observer* for 34 years.

St Dunstan-in-the-West

St Dunstan's shape is perfect for its role as both an Anglican and a Romanian Orthodox church. There is an alcove for the Anglican altar and another for the Orthodox iconostasis brought from the Antim Monastery in Bucharest. This association dates from Archbishop Michael Ramsey's visit to Romania in 1965. Since 2003 this has also been the Diocese of London's church for Europe and the number of Orthodox worshippers has grown following the admission of Romania to the EU.

The Western and Orthodox calendar differences mean that Easter is sometimes celebrated twice and some weeks apart.

Open Monday to Friday 11am to 2pm
Fleet Street EC4A 2HR
www.stdunstaninthewest.org

30
St Ethelburga's, Bishopsgate
Anglican

Bishopsgate has a hint of New York because the office blocks are so tall that they dwarf the City of London's smallest church. The interior varies depending on whether there is a meeting, concert or service.

This is the only church dedicated to Ethelburga, sister of St Erconwald and first Abbess of Barking, who died in about 676. It was founded in 1230 and the 1400 rebuild that survived the Great Fire was described by John Betjeman as 'the best example of a medieval parish church in the City'.

In 1607 Henry Hudson, of Hudson Bay fame, and his crew attended a Holy Communion service before setting sail in search of the North West Passage.

High-profile rectors include Blessed John Larke who, like one of his parishioners St Thomas More, was martyred for opposing Henry VIII's break with Rome. Luke Milburne was attacked in print by Alexander Pope for criticizing John Dryden. Dr William Geikie-Cobb was incumbent from 1900 to 1941 and became notorious for marrying divorcees who had been refused elsewhere.

The much admired simple Kentish ragstone frontage with its small doorway has not always been familiar to Londoners. For several centuries, from 1570 to 1932, it was hidden by a narrow building which in the early twentieth century was an optician's premises.

The church's present role as a centre for reconciliation and peace is the result of an IRA bomb that exploded nearby on a Saturday morning in April 1993. The church was almost completely demolished with just the east end and south side arcading left standing. Amazingly, the Hans Feibusch mural behind the altar survived as did Pieter Coecke van Aelst's painting *Christ Healing Blind Bartimaeus*, which had been removed for cleaning.

The centre, the idea of Bishop of London Richard Chartres, was opened in 2002 and offers a programme of lectures, discussions and debates involving Christians, Jews, Muslims and members of other faiths and none. This is not an inappropriate use as two of its rectors have been very aware of non-Christian culture. William Bedwell, who was asked in 1604 to help with the translation for the King James Bible, compiled an Arab lexicon and translated diplomatic letters for James I. John Rodwell, rector from 1843 to 1900 and pioneer Anglo-Catholic, made the first English translation of the Quran.

St Ethelburga's, Bishopsgate

Behind the church there is a Bedouin tent made of woven goats hair used for meetings and claimed as the only place in London where faith representatives can meet on equal terms and not as a guest of another.

This remains an Anglican church with the font by the front door and a cross, made from nails that were once part of the bombed Coventry Cathedral, on the altar. There is a monthly Eucharist and a service on St Ethelburga's Day – 12 October. But the chairs are exceedingly comfortable for a church.

Open Fridays 11am to 3pm
Bishopsgate EC2N 4AG
www.stethelburgas.org

31

St Etheldreda's, Ely Place

Roman Catholic

The church is found beyond the forbidding gates of a private road off Holborn Circus. The upper church, lit by some of London's largest stained glass windows, is reached by way of a cloister and a stone staircase.

The building dates from 1252 and is London's only pre-Reformation church still in Roman Catholic use. It began as the chapel of the Bishop of Ely's London residence. Its garden is now Hatton Garden. The Mitre pub, in a linking passage, is a remnant of the house. The dedication is to Ely Cathedral's founder, St Etheldreda.

The chapel is built on two levels. The tiled cloister gave us the term 'a night on the tiles' after the bishop held a five-day party for Henry VIII. It was here that Henry later discussed divorce from Katharine of Aragon with Archbishop Cranmer.

The King took over the house at the Reformation but under James I the chapel was briefly used again for Roman Catholic worship when borrowed by the Spanish Embassy. During the nineteenth century it was occupied by Welsh Anglicans, until 1873 when it was purchased by Fr William Crockhart and given to the Rosminians in whose care it remains. John Francis Bentley designed a west end screen.

During World War Two, four beams crashed down during bombing. Only the crypt remained open and it was here that Douglas Hyde, editor of the communist *Daily Worker*, experienced conversion. The church re-opened in 1952 with a glorious east window by Joseph Nuttgens. The west window by Charles Blakeman features Reformation martyrs who passed close to here on their way to execution. Mary Nuttgens created the eight statues of martyrs high up on medieval corbels.

Statue of Etheldreda in the crypt

St Etheldreda's, Ely Place

Visitors stream in on St Blaise's Day, 3 February, when the traditional blessing of throats is available, and St Etheldreda's Day on 23 June.

Weddings at this church noted for good music include journalist Hugo Young and 7/7 survivor Gill Hicks. The funeral of author Alice Thomas Ellis was held here in 2005 when The Keys, the Catholic writers' guild, still met in the crypt. It remains a favourite church of Princess Michael of Kent who worshipped here when first in London.

The outstanding rector for 32 years, until 2008, was Kit Cunningham who acted as chaplain to Fleet Street, edited the diocesan newspaper, opened the cafe in the cloister and founded an annual Strawberrie Fayre inspired by Shakespeare's reference in *Richard III* to 'good strawberries' in the garden. Fr Kit was assisted by Rosemary Nibbs who had once been the secretary of playwright Joe Orton. The team also included Fr Jean Charles-Roux, the colourful French royalist and brother-in-law of French politician Gaston Defferre.

In 1985 the altar was subtly moved forward to allow the priest to stand on either side without spoiling the feel of the sanctuary. In 2009 a new organ was installed by the Swiss firm Späth.

Open daily
Ely Place, Holborn Circus EC1N 6RY
www.stetheldreda.com

32

Farm Street Church, Mayfair

Roman Catholic

This church is known by its entrance in Farm Street which recalls the time when the site was Hay Hill Farm. This is the best way to enter although for convenience many go in from the higher level Mount Street Gardens where a brick arcade gives little clue to the lovely gothic revival church with fine east and west windows down below.

The rarely mentioned dedication is to the Immaculate Conception chosen five years before Pope IX defined the dogma in 1854. The church, built soon after the Catholic Emancipation Act as part of the English Jesuit mother house, has a west front (which is really south) modelled on a transept of Beauvais Cathedral in France.

Inside there is no screen to spoil the clear view down to a Pugin altar below an 'east' window based on the one at Carlisle Cathedral. The problem with having a freestanding altar has been solved by creating a replica of Pugin's original which remains in place behind, along with his reredos.

The church, by J. J. Scoles, is highly decorated for the 1840s but more was to come. The side aisles and chapels are by Henry Clutton, Romaine Walker and A. E. Purdie. The roundels between the nave arches were only finished with mosaics in 1996. The round west window, damaged in World War Two, has glass by Evie Hone. It has deep colours but the church is not dark.

When built, this was London's leading Roman Catholic church predating the London Oratory and Westminster Cathedral. Anglican Henry Manning came for instruction. Evelyn Waugh was received here in 1930 and returned for Edith Sitwell's conversion, which was celebrated afterwards across the road at The Connaught with Alec Guinness. In 1889 the Prince of Wales attended the requiem for Archduke Rudolf of Austria who had been found shot dead at Mayerling.

The great Jesuit names associated with this church include Ronald Knox, Martin D'Arcy, Bernard Basset, Tom Corbishley, Peter Hebblethwaite and Peter Knott. In residence for many postwar years after being Archbishop of Bombay was the progressive Thomas Roberts who supported CND.

As the Jesuit HQ this was a church mainly for Mass with great preaching. It was said that it was 'hard to see the high altar for the sea of mink coats' but, although situated in fashionable Mayfair, there were never any weddings. This changed in

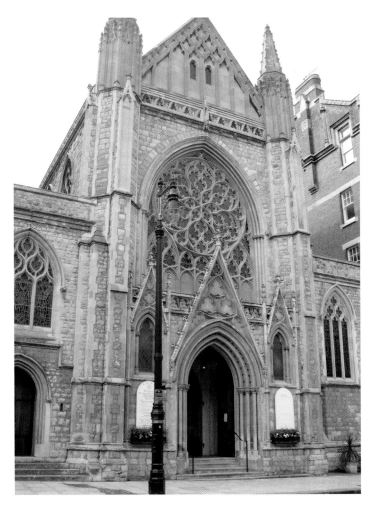

Farm Street Church, Mayfair

1966 when Farm Street became a parish church. A baptistry had to be created and the Ignatius Chapel is soundproofed as a refuge for crying babies. A family Mass has its own children's liturgy of the word.

There is very thick carpet, which must make wedding couples feel as if they are walking on air but allows children to run through the delightful arcading without causing a disturbance. It is just possible, when the church is very quiet, to detect a rumble from the Jubilee Line.

Open daily 7am to 7.30pm
Mount Street w1k 3ah
www.farmstreet.org.uk

33
St Francis, Pottery Lane
Roman Catholic

The brick church on the corner of Pottery Lane and Hippodrome Place in Notting Dale is one of the older Roman Catholic churches in London.

The tight site, which does not allow for the usual east–west alignment, was chosen by Cardinal Henry Manning who knew of the poor Irish living in the former potteries. A large kiln survives just north of the church. Henry Clutton designed the first church which was opened at Candlemas 1860. It was paid for by the first priest Henry Rawes and the worshippers were survivors of a cholera epidemic.

But at once it proved too small and Clutton's pupil J. F. Bentley, who had supervised the work, was ask to expand it. He added the Lady Chapel, cleverly placed beyond and slightly behind the high altar. In 1862 Bentley, the future architect of Westminster Cathedral, was the first to be baptized in his splendid vaulted baptistry described at the time as 'one of the most complete little chapels in England'. Bentley's second name at his christening (Francis) was from this church's dedication.

The statue of Our Lady is by Theodore Phyffers who had been brought from Antwerp by Pugin to work at the new Palace of Westminster. The 1870 stations of the cross by Nathaniel H. J. Westlake run along the wall like a quality strip cartoon.

The small church has the feel of a grotto with its rich vaulted 'east end' but it is not dark thanks to the off-white walls. Thick blue fitted carpet keeps the noise down and creates a 'holy quiet'.

Bentley also designed the clergy house and school which helps to create a pleasant courtyard outside. Here there is a bust of St Francis of Assisi by sculptor Arthur Fleischman. It was blessed by Bishop Agnellus Andrew, who had a familiar voice having been the regular commentator for the broadcasts of the Pope's Easter Blessing.

Until 2000 the parish priest was the popular Oliver McTernan, regularly heard on Radio 4's *Thought for the Day*, and whose leadership owed much to his positive interpretation of the Second Vatican Council teaching.

The poor in the parish have largely been replaced by the families of professional people who since the 1960s have spread west down the hill from Ladbroke Grove.

St Francis' courtyard, Pottery Lane

But recently the church provided a refuge for immigrants brought to London as 'slave labour', and today the Catholic Geez Rite Chaplaincy serving Ethiopians is also based here.

The church has a long list of people who are welcome ('all faiths and cultures, divorced or separated person . . .') and what is celebrated ('diversity, a spirit of hospitality, the unity that God wills . . . '). The main Mass on Sunday, which has boy and girl servers, is packed with people standing at the back. Afterwards coffee is available in the former school which has become the community centre. There is daily Mass and sometimes an evening Mass with Taizé chants.

Open daily 8.30am to 5.30pm
Pottery Lane, Notting Hill W11 4NQ
www.rcdow.org.uk/nottinghill

34
St George's, Bloomsbury

Anglican

The church has an extraordinary tower topped by a statue of George I on a pyramid with a lion and unicorn playfully gripping the base. Horace Walpole called it 'a masterpiece of absurdity'.

This was the last of the six churches designed by Nicholas Hawksmoor and the last built under the Fifty Churches Act. It is the only Hawksmoor church to be spared war damage.

Hawksmoor modelled the pyramid on descriptions of the tomb of Mausolus at Hallicarnassus, one of the seven wonders of the world, whose sculptures are in the British Museum in the parish. The church's deep Corinthian portico appears to have been inspired by the Roman Temple of Bacchus at Baalbek in the Lebanon. Surprisingly, it was not intended as the main entrance.

The architect won the commission by insisting that he could design an east–west church for the difficult site. The church opened in 1731, 17 years after George I's death. An early view of the steeple is found in Hogarth's *Gin Lane*. But by 1781 there were calls for more seats and the orientation was changed to north–south.

From 1956 to 1968 this was the University of London's chapel. From 1991 to 1995 priest-in-charge and artist Michael Day made it a focus for a chaplaincy to art colleges with a celebration on St Dunstan's Day. A small part of the crypt was used for art exhibitions including one by Churton Fairman. By the new century the church was on both the English Heritage Buildings at Risk register and the World Monuments Fund 100 Most Endangered Sites list.

But in 2008 the interior was re-ordered as Hawksmoor intended as part of a £9.4 million restoration funded by the Paul Mellon Estate, the Heritage Lottery Fund and other donors.

The four-year restoration was under the direction of Colin Kerr of Molyneux Kerr Architects who took the decision to return the building to its original state. Blocked windows now have glass, and stained glass windows have clear glass. Victorian pews have been replaced with oak benches on a new stone surface with underfloor heating.

A gallery has been built on the north side so that once more galleries, as for the Dukes of Bedford and Montagu, face each other.

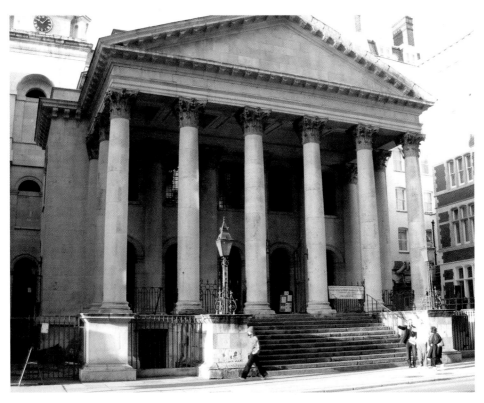

St George's, Bloomsbury

Memorials include one under the tower to Charles Grant, Chairman of the East India Company and friend of William Wilberforce.

The crypt has been cleared of bodies, allowing the space to be occupied by a permanent multimedia exhibition on Hawksmoor and Bloomsbury.

Early baptisms include author Anthony Trollope and Cowley Fathers' founder Richard Benson.

Special occasions include the funeral in 1913 of suffragette Emily Davison who threw herself under the King's horse at the Derby. The rector Charles Baumgarten had suggested that 'women's influence might enrich the nation'. His successor William Roberts was an early supporter of women's ordination. In 1937 Emperor Haile Selassie of Ethiopia was present at a Requiem Mass for those killed during the Abyssinian War.

There is a Sunday Mass, weekday lunchtime services and regular concerts.

Open 1pm to 4pm
Bloomsbury Way WC1E 6DP
www.stgeorgesbloomsbury.org.uk

35

St George the Martyr, Borough

Anglican

The steeple is the landmark for visitors looking south down Southwark's Borough High Street. Inside, this is a Georgian church steeped in history stretching back more than its visible 250 years.

St George's stands on the site of a Roman building at a rare bend in Watling Street and has Roman bricks in the base of its tower. The first mention of the church is in 1122. It was rebuilt in gothic style in about 1390 when it was known to poet John Gower who included the new church in his will.

This was the building seen by Henry V in 1415 when he stopped on his way back from victory at Agincourt where St George had been invoked. The King's first act was to insist that the status of St George's Day was raised to that of a major feast. On Henry's death his funeral procession to Westminster Abbey began here with the singing of a solemn dirge.

William Hogarth's *Southwark Fair* etching shows the church in 1732 just before it was demolished to be rebuilt in its present smaller form. The foundation stone was laid on St George's Day in 1734 and the work had only just been completed when architect John Price died in 1736. The ceiling includes the arms of the Skinners, Drapers, Fishmongers and Glovers livery companies who donated to the building fund.

This is often called the Little Dorrit Church because Charles Dickens, in his *Little Dorrit,* describes Amy sleeping in front of the vestry fireplace with the burial register for a pillow. She also marries here and is now depicted in a corner of the east window.

The church is built on gravel and the first sign that the building could eventually collapse was detected in 1938. When the poet laureate Andrew Motion gave a talk in 2000 the audience was asked to sit round the edge of the church in case the ceiling fell down. Now a restoration has floated the building on a concrete table.

Those buried here, and reburied to enable restoration, include Nahum Tate who wrote the carol 'While shepherds watched their flocks by

Little Dorrit window

St George the Martyr, Borough

night' and Andrew Stoney of 'stoney broke' fame, whose wife Mary Bowes was great-great grandmother of Queen Elizabeth The Queen Mother.

Married here in 1654 during the dark days of the Civil War was General Monck who was the first to greet Charles II on his return to England. The royal arms displayed are from the Stuart period.

Among the rectors are Henry VIII's secretary Peter Carmelianus, mathematician Edmund Gunter of 'Gunter's Chain' fame, and Pepys' friend Hezekiah Burton.

Today the church is the focus for the St George in Southwark Festival on St George's Day. The annual Dickens Fellowship Service is followed by a lunch when the rector says grace using the words of Charles Dickens. Daily services are sometimes attended by staff from the USPG offices opposite. A new undercroft created by the restoration provides space for conferences and community events.

Open Saturday mornings
Borough High Street SE1 1JD
www.stgeorge-themartyr.co.uk

36
St George's, Hanover Square

Anglican

This church dominates George Street, with its pillared portico reaching out over the pavement and into the road. The warm galleried interior has more elegant columns and William Kent's *Last Supper* as the focus at the east end.

The church was built in the 1720s for a parish being carved out of St Martin-in-the-Fields whose own new church was rising at the same time. Architect John James, working here on a much tighter budget, produced a similar building.

Although not an ancient church site, the east windows are sixteenth century. The surprise Flemish glass was made for a church in Antwerp and placed here in 1840 although St George has replaced an image of the Holy Roman Emperor Charles V who is now found at Wilton Church in Wiltshire.

Round the gallery are displayed the names of churchwardens, many of whom are titled – such as the Earl of Radnor and Lord Salisbury.

In 1816 the church hosted over 1,000 weddings with nine on Christmas Day. Even *The Adventures of Sherlock Holmes* features a wedding here. Those marrying at St George's include the original clown Joseph Grimaldi, poet P. B. Shelley, Prime Ministers Benjamin Disraeli and Herbert Asquith, President Franklin D. Roosevelt, writer George Eliot, and radio inventor Marconi. One royal wedding proved a disaster as George III's son, the Duke of Sussex, had failed to obtain his father's permission. Although the couple remained together, the marriage was officially annulled.

It was still known as the 'weddings church' when William Atkins, rector for 45 years, arrived in 1955. For his first five years he continued as Librarian of St Paul's and later he was also chaplain to the Réunion des Gastronomes. Aged 84, he was asked by the bishop if he had a retirement date in mind. 'No,' he replied, 'I have never regarded this as a temporary appointment.'

Although devoted to the Book of Common Prayer, William Atkins was prepared to lead the way with change and successfully replaced Sunday matins with a Sung Eucharist. The only loss regretted during his incumbency was that of the two stone dogs, seated pointers, who had sat outside the church since 1940 and mysteriously disappeared one night.

A plaque records Handel living in nearby Brook Street from 1723 to 1759 and attending the new church. He advised on the organ installation and helped select

St George's, Hanover Square

the first organist. Today there is an annual Handel Festival and regular lunchtime concerts. Pew rents may have gone but pew sponsorship allows exclusive use of the pew at two concerts a year.

Every Advent since 1978 there has been a presentation by leading public figures of 'The Story of Christmas', a ticketed lessons and carols festival, which raises money for children and the homeless. Dame Judi Dench heads such celebrities as Katie Derham, Ian Hislop and Aled Jones.

Open Monday to Friday 8am to 4pm
St George Street W1S 1FX
www.stgeorgeshanoversquare.org

37
St Giles-in-the-Fields, St Giles High Street

Anglican

The church lies almost below the high-rise Centrepoint but hides a large churchyard and a community garden. John Betjeman called the present interior 'one of the most successful post war restorations'.

St Giles is the patron of lepers and the origin of this church is a chapel built on the site in 1101 as part of a leper hospital founded by Henry I's wife, Queen Matilda. The institution was dissolved by Henry VIII in 1539, leaving the chapel to become a parish church that was soon known as St Giles-in-the-Fields.

At this time it was the last stop for condemned prisoners on their way from Newgate Prison in the City to Tyburn gallows. Many Reformation martyrs came here and 11 were brought back from execution to be buried in the churchyard. All were beatified and one, Oliver Plunket, has been canonized. His body is now at Downside Abbey near Bath while his head is at Drogheda in Ireland.

The church was rebuilt in 1630 when nearby Covent Garden's new church was being completed. The present St Giles and its fine Vestry House were finished in 1734, having been designed by Henry Flitcroft, architect of Woburn Abbey.

The Moses and Aaron paintings on each side of the altar are by Francisco Vieira the younger, the King of Portugal's court painter.

A spare pulpit is from the nearby West Street Chapel where it was used by John and Charles Wesley. Robert Browning and Elizabeth Barrett were married in 1845 before the south aisle altar when it stood in St Marylebone Church.

Buried here are George Herbert's brother Edward, the poet Andrew Marvell, William Balmain who arrived with the first fleet in New South Wales and gave his name to a Sydney suburb, and House of Commons printer Luke Hansard.

At the back of the church there is a plaque to the second Lord Baltimore which was unveiled as recently as 1996 by the Governor of Maryland in the presence of the American Ambassador. Lord Baltimore, who was buried here in 1675, governed from London as the first Proprietary of Maryland. The colony was founded in 1634 when ships arrived carrying passengers who included parishioners of St Giles.

There are also memorials to George Chapman, who first translated Homer, and sculptor John Flaxman.

St Giles-in-the-Fields, St Giles High Street

Christenings include John Milton's daughter Mary in 1647, and on the same day in 1818 Shelley's children William and Clara and Byron's daughter Allegra. Playwright John Osborne's memorial service was held here.

The Prayer Book tradition was established by Gordon Taylor, rector for 51 years until 1999, who revived the bombed church and parish life. On Sundays there is Choral Matins and Choral Eucharist. There are regular Friday lunchtime recitals. The annual Tyburn Walk in honour of the Roman Catholic Martyrs pauses here, and the Corpus Christi procession from St Patrick's in Soho Square joins the evensong congregation for Benediction in the churchyard.

Open Monday to Friday 9am to 4pm
St Giles High Street WC2H 8LG
www.stgilesonline.org

38
Grosvenor Chapel, South Audley Street
Anglican

This is a New England building in Mayfair with a colourful flower stall against its wall and a garden at the back.

The foundation stone of the brick chapel for a new housing estate was laid in 1730 by landowner Sir Richard Grosvenor. The porch covers the pavement, as at the nearby St George's in Hanover Square, which was known to the builder, Benjamin Timbrell. He had worked with Gibbs on the similar St Peter, Vere Street.

The Grosvenor Chapel is a small galleried church with clear windows and, thanks to a screen with Ionic pillars inserted by Comper in front of the original chancel, even more intimate than first intended.

Beyond the screen, the east end has become a Lady Chapel with a hanging pyx. Box pews survive in the three-sided gallery where there is London's 'most authentically Enlightenment organ' rebuilt recently in the original 1732 case.

This only ceased to be a proprietary chapel and to come under the parish church of St George in 1829. Until recently, the priest was still known as 'chaplain'.

Buried here in the vault is writer and traveller Lady Mary Wortley Montagu who had a quiet funeral on the day after her death in 1762. Also here is radical politician John Wilkes who urged recognition of American independence. This is appropriate since the building is contemporary with so many American churches and is now the nearest Episcopalian church to the US Embassy which is in the same street. General Eisenhower attended the church during World War Two when it was the American Forces Chapel.

Chaplains include Thomas Newton who was Dean of St Paul's from 1768 to 1782, and Henry Wace who was Dean of Canterbury from 1904 to 1924. Dick Sheppard was here for a year before going to St Martin-in-the-Fields. Bishop Charles Gore assisted during his retirement years and his book *Christian Moral Principles* began here as Lenten sermons preached in 1921. John Betjeman described the 1970s' chaplain John Gaskell as 'the best preacher in England'.

The congregation has included the Duke of Wellington, Florence Nightingale and Princess Margaret. Author Rose Macaulay came to Mass daily. More recently, Princess Michael has come to support fundraising.

Grosvenor Chapel, South Audley Street

Americans come in force for their Thanksgiving service in November and a few weeks later the church is again crowded for the fundraising candlelit carol concert followed by a reception at a prestigious address. On Palm Sunday there is a joint blessing of palms with the Farm Street congregation in the adjoining Mount Street Gardens.

A professional ensemble of five voices sings a Mass setting on Sunday morning when there is a congregation of at least 50 in otherwise empty Mayfair. A thriving Sunday school meets in the Garden Room of the attached house on the north-east corner. This is a former school built in 1841 which is also used for receptions. There are weekday lunchtime concerts.

Open Monday to Friday 9.30am to 1pm
South Audley Street W1K 2PA
www.grosvenorchapel.org.uk

39
Guy's Chapel, St Thomas Street

Anglican and Roman Catholic

The chapel, sandwiched between the houses built for the Guy's Hospital superintendent and matron, looks like a residence. It is entered through a narrow front door below the main hospital clock and in the 'entrance hall' blue carpeted stairs on two sides sweep up to the gallery of the square church.

This terrace with a chapel in the middle, on one side of a Georgian courtyard, was designed by Richard Rupp and built between 1774 and 1780. Outside is a statue of hospital founder Thomas Guy who was a controversial eccentric with a fortune made from printing Bibles without authority and selling investments before the burst of the 'South Sea Bubble'. Having fallen out with his fellow governors of St Thomas' Hospital who would not admit 'incurables', he founded his own hospital across the road from which no one would ever be turned away. He died in 1724 two years before any patients were admitted.

Most dominant in the chapel is not the altar but a large and very fine white marble monument to Thomas Guy by John Bacon. It shows Thomas Guy inviting

Thomas Guy monument

a stricken figure into the hospital which is seen in relief in the background. An inscription includes the claim that 'He established this Asylum for that stage of Languor and Disease to which the Charities of Others had not reached'.

The windows above the altar are a memorial to silk merchant and benefactor William Hunt whose name lives on with New Hunt's House built in 1999 to house the Guy's, King's and St Thomas' Schools of Biomedical Sciences, Medicine and Dentistry. Other memorials include one for William Gladstone, who was a Guy's Hospital governor, and the physician Thomas Addison of Addison's Disease fame.

A recent addition is a new icon of Jesus and Mary, which now forms the focus of a prayer area used by medical students and hospital visitors.

The crypt houses the tomb of Thomas Guy whose body was brought from

Guy's Chapel

St Thomas Church opposite some 50 years after his death to be reburied in his own hospital. Surgeon and scientist Astley Cooper, who died in 1841 and whose students included the poet John Keats, was at his own request also buried in the crypt.

Keats, who knew the chapel in 1815 and 1816 when he lodged just outside the gates at 28 St Thomas Street with Astley Cooper's dresser, has recently been remembered in effigy seated in a former London Bridge alcove in the colonnade leading into the courtyard.

This, the original hospital chapel, is now part of the Guy's campus of King's College and served by two chaplains attached to King's. Both the Anglican Eucharist and Roman Catholic Mass are celebrated during the week. Among the popular annual services are the All Souls Day Mass in the crypt and the carol service, both of which are candlelit.

The grand piano offers opportunities for occasional lunchtime recitals.

Open daily
St Thomas Street SE1 9RT
www.kcl.ac.uk

40
Harrow-on-the-Hill Church

Anglican

The church is a landmark in Middlesex and its churchyard affords a panoramic view across central London to the skyscrapers at Canary Wharf and those in the City.

Archbishop Lanfranc, who owned the Harrow manor, started the building of the first St Mary's Church in 1087, and seven years later it was consecrated by his successor St Anselm just a month after he had become primate.

A visitor to the church during its first century was Thomas Becket who was at his estate here less than a fortnight before his murder in Canterbury Cathedral at Christmas 1170. The Harrow clergy, having taken the side of the King, were hostile to their archbishop and gave him only a cool welcome.

The tower base is Norman but much of the main church is the work of the thirteenth-century rector Canon Elias de Dereham who had been a strong supporter of Magna Carta and assisted in distributing copies around the country. Being involved in the building of Salisbury Cathedral he is credited with influencing the spread of English gothic architecture. John Byrkhehe, appointed rector in 1437, was also a master builder and he installed the magnificent roof with carvings.

The north door is Norman along with the font. A chest in the north transept also dates from this period. The magnificent carved wooden pulpit with a canopy is seventeenth century. The east window is by Comper.

Monuments include one by Flaxman to farmer John Lyon who founded Harrow School in 1572 and is buried below. Also commemorated is bookseller James Edwards who in 1816 was buried in a coffin made out of his own oak bookshelves.

The building was given a makeover by George Gilbert Scott during the years 1846–9 when the outside walls were faced with flint and battlements added. He also reconstructed the chapel above the porch which is reached by steep wooden stairs inside.

In the churchyard, entered through a lychgate, is the 'Peachey Stone' on which Byron used to lie gazing at the view when a Harrow schoolboy. He loved the spot so much that his daughter Allegra is buried outside the church door in an unmarked grave.

Also here is a tombstone of Thomas Port who died in 1838 and was the first

Harrow-on-the-Hill Church

person to be killed by a railway train in public service. Less than a century later the road outside the church was the scene of the first car accident fatality.

Diplomat Cuthbert Tunstall was rector from 1511 and resided here as much as his overseas trips allowed before becoming Bishop of London in 1522.

Lord Shaftesbury's resolve to involve himself in charitable work began here when as a schoolboy he saw two drunks, carrying a pauper's coffin, stagger up the hill and drop it before reaching the church.

The church is sustained by parishioners rather than Harrow School and maintains both a strong choir and a thriving Sunday school.

Open daily
Church Hill HA1 3HL
www.harrowhill.org

41
St Helen's, Bishopsgate

Anglican

The west end of the church has two front doors and an interior that is exceptionally large.

There was originally a Norman church here and in about 1204 a Benedictine convent was built on the north side, with its chapel immediately alongside the parish church.

The wide building today is the result of the parallel churches being rebuilt together with just a wooden screen separating the naves. Most of the walls are thirteenth century. A transept on the south side was added in the fourteenth century and the double nave church was much improved in 1480 when the central arches were added. The high windows on the north side allowed for the now lost convent cloister to abut at ground level. The religious community was evicted in 1538.

The look of the church today is the result of a dramatic restoration and re-ordering following severe damage caused by an IRA bomb exploding nearby in 1992. Glass splinters from office blocks lay like snow inside and out while insurance documents blew in the wind for days. The following year another bomb, which demolished much of nearby St Ethelburga's, shook the church.

The restoration proposals by architect Quinlan Terry were so controversial that a nine-day sitting of a consistory court was necessary before work could begin. The church has been given just one floor level, higher than before, which allows for underfloor heating and cabling. This is best understood by visiting the Spencer tomb where one now looks down rather than up on the recumbent couple. The walls have been painted cream and a new Georgian-style balcony added at the west end. Although there are more monuments here than in any other City church, there is a minimalist feel.

The Pearson chancel screen has been relocated to be just a screen and pews are replaced by chairs. The focus is not now on the east end but the early seventeenth-century pulpit on the south side. The communion table, between occasional use, is hidden in the transept behind Sir John Crosby's tomb. His equally ancient house, which stood in the parish, was moved to Chelsea.

In the nuns' choir, where fifteenth-century stalls survive, is the tomb of Gresham College founder Sir Thomas Gresham. A sword rest has the arms of Sir John Lawrence who, as Lord Mayor, remained at his house in the parish during the

St Helen's, Bishopsgate

1665 Great Plague. The convent nave's east window by Quinlan Terry includes old glass. Another window recalls William Shakespeare who lived in the parish shortly before the Globe was relocated from nearby Shoreditch to Southwark.

This is a seriously evangelical church which maybe explains why the Lady Chapel has been allowed to disappear with refurbishment. The congregation for the Tuesday Talk, a series begun in 1962 by rector Dick Lucas, is always packed and larger than the Sunday one which still manages to attract a high number of families and students.

Open Monday to Friday with entry via the church office
Great St Helen's, Bishopsgate EC3A 6AT
www.st-helens.org.uk

42

Holy Redeemer, Clerkenwell

Anglican

The Most Holy Redeemer Church is an Italian basilica planted in hilltop Exmouth Market overlooking Farringdon. It is a delightful part of the streetscape and looks its best during a baking hot lunchtime with busy stalls in the traffic-free street and Mass being celebrated beyond the open doors.

Behind the church are the remains of Spa Fields which run up to the east wall. The church site was once occupied by the Spa Fields Chapel which was for a time the main focus of the Countess of Huntington's sect.

The first vicar, Edward Eyre, did not want 'cheap gothic' so he was fortunate to be able to work with architect J. D. Sedding, churchwarden of nearby St Alban's in Holborn. William Gladstone laid the foundation stone in 1887 and the church, with its gabled front and impressive eaves, was consecrated the following year. The campanile was added in 1906 by architect Henry Wilson who had worked on the church with Sedding.

The building, which has the Latin inscription *Christo Liberatori* (To Christ the Redeemer) across the front, is based on Santo Spirito in Florence. Light comes from clear glass round windows that are mainly high up.

The dominant feature inside is a huge *baldachino* surmounted by the figure of 'The Living Christ And Yet The Crucified' designed by Wilson in 1927 as a memorial to Fr Eyre. Unusually, the original altar below remains in use since no facing altar has been introduced.

The many pictures are copies of Italian masters painted over 30 years by regular worshipper Lillian Reynolds. The statues of St Pancras and the Blessed Virgin flanking the Lady Chapel altar represent former parish guilds for boys and girls.

The Chapel of All Souls was completed in 1922 to Wilson's design as a memorial to those who died in World War One. The organ was once in Windsor Castle's chapel.

The altarpiece and candlesticks in the St Mary Magdalene Chapel come from Holy Redeemer's former mother church, St Philip Granville Square, which closed just before World War Two.

The tradition is catholic with care taken regarding daily liturgy. The church has a fine collection of vestments. Candles burn at the Sacred Heart and Our Lady of Walsingham altars and the St George statue.

Holy Redeemer, Clerkenwell

The small parish has seen huge changes. Ethnic food stalls have appeared to feed lunchtime workers, and the vicar has said that he cannot now afford to eat in some of the restaurants. Today's poor are those who trail past the church on their way to or from one of the nearby immigration courts.

An overwhelmingly local congregation of about 60 attends Sunday's High Mass. A Junior Church meets on Sunday morning and includes children who also attend the parish school.

Highlights of the parish year are the street processions led by a brass band on Palm Sunday and at the Holy Redeemer festival on 15 July, which elsewhere is St Swithun's Day.

Open mornings
Exmouth Market EC1R 4QE
www.holyredeemer.co.uk

43
Holy Trinity, Dalston

Anglican

The dark brick Victorian church with a tower rising over Dalston is a focus for both parishioners and a large number of visitors.

Building took place during 1878 and 1879. The architect was Ewan Christian, brother-in-law of J. L. Pearson and a close friend and executor of S. S. Teulon, whose influence can be seen in the massive tower. Christian's most famous building is the National Portrait Gallery which he worked on later in life.

Following a serious fire in 1985 the church interior is now whitewashed, the sanctuary being especially bright, and the pews have been replaced with red chairs. The screen with painted figures comes from demolished St Philip's, Dalston.

Holy Trinity's vicar in the 1950s was leading Christian socialist Stanley Evans, known for his writing, preaching and support for CND, and in 1959 he agreed to the annual clown service being held here. The tradition had started in 1946 at St James's, Pentonville Road, which is depicted in John O'Connor's famous 1884 painting *From Pentonville Road looking west: evening*. The first clown, Joseph Grimaldi (1778–1837), is buried in its churchyard.

But clowns even in ordinary clothes were not made very welcome at St James's which subsequently closed. The replacement building is secular but has an exterior similar in outline to the church.

The clown service at Holy Trinity is on the first Sunday in February during the entertainment industry's quiet period which once followed the Christmas circus performances at Earls Court, Haringey Arena and Olympia and the summer season. The custom of clowns wearing costume to church only began in 1967. Now the always very well-attended service with clowns and visitors from home and abroad does not just eclipse Candlemas at the beginning of the month but affects the whole life of the building all year.

There is a stained glass window depicting Grimaldi above a quotation from Ecclesiastes: 'A time to weep, a time to laugh, a time to mourn, a time to dance'. A huge banner carries the words 'Here we are fools for Christ'.

Also at the church are examples of clown faces recorded on eggshells as in the Clowns International archive. At the service clowns not only lay a wreath for Grimaldi but also recall clowns who have died during the past year. A free show for children follows in the hall.

Holy Trinity, Dalston

Just as the church has changed its interior and churchmanship since its opening in 1897 so the parish housing has changed dramatically. Even the name of the street outside the church has changed from Mayfield Road to Beechwood Road.

But for all the international attention this is still a parish church with a multicultural congregation at the Sung Eucharist on Sunday, children from the school opposite coming for a weekly assembly, and a Friday youth club.

Open on the first Friday of the month noon to 5pm
Beechwood Road E8 3DY
www.clowns-international.com

44
Holy Trinity, Sloane Square
Anglican

The red brick church, hinting at King's College Chapel in Cambridge, is in Sloane Street where it stands behind impressive railings as a superb example of Arts and Crafts architecture and decoration.

Building started in 1888 on the site given by the Earl of Cadogan who at the time was Lord Privy Seal in Lord Salisbury's government. The Earl also financed both the building designed by Anglo-Catholic J. D. Sedding and its fittings by great craftsmen of the day.

Inside there is a very wide nave with an east window depicting almost 50 saints by Sir Edward Burne-Jones and William Morris. Sedding died before the church's completion but his assistant Henry Wilson masterminded, as the architect intended, the interior decoration along with other members of the Art Workers Guild.

The chancel screen is marble with wrought iron gates. The style of the building is perpendicular but the pulpit and Lady Chapel have red marble columns. A lectern, in memory of the Countess of Cadogan, is a unique design by John Williams of Hornsey.

The red and blue of the St Michael and Gabriel windows in the Memorial Chapel are incredibly rich and subtle even on a dull day.

Holy Trinity, east window

Composer John Ireland, who wrote the melody for the hymn 'My song is love unknown', was assistant organist when both he and the church were young.

In the 1950s, after urgent postwar repair, there were still pew rents and sidesmen would ask visitors not to sit in a rented pew. Attendance dwindled after the departure in 1980 of Alfred Carver who had been vicar for 35 years. The church, called the 'Cathedral of the Arts & Crafts Movement' by John Betjeman, was in danger of becoming a little visited museum.

Holy Trinity remains open and with a growing congregation thanks to the decade-long ministry of Michael Marshall who in 1997

Holy Trinity, Sloane Square

became 'Bishop in Residence' at a church on the verge of closure. The former Bishop of Woolwich insisted on having the doors open all day and described his time here as the 'happiest chapter in my whole ministry'.

The church has always had a catholic tradition. Sedding was churchwarden at St Alban's in Holborn. John Keble is depicted alongside St Martin and St Nicholas. Today Holy Trinity claims to be 'modern catholic' with a mission of both critical and compassionate Christianity.

There is a Sung Eucharist and Junior Church every Sunday, unlike in earlier years when August saw a severe reduction in services. Trinity Sunday is kept as a vibrant festival with a procession to Sloane Square. One year saw a release of 308 balloons representing each member of the congregation.

Other new annual events include the Chelsea Schubert Festival. The use of chairs rather than pews allows for the nave to be a flexible space.

The parish is a long narrow buffer running from the top of Sloane Street in Knightsbridge to Royal Hospital Road. Its primary school is at the back of the church in Sedding Street.

Open daily
Sloane Street SW1X 9BZ
www.holytrinitysloanesquare.co.uk

45
Isleworth Church
Anglican

This 1960s church sits surprisingly successfully at the base of an old tower in a superb riverside village setting. The new square church is approached through the open-air nave of the old church.

The site, on which stood a Saxon church, is on slightly raised ground above a wall where tablets record flooding. The church tower is fifteenth century. The nave, which had been rebuilt in 1708, stands roofless due to a fire in 1943. This was not war damage but arson by boys, which shocked the parish.

It was 20 years before an architect was appointed. The eventual choice was Michael Blee, a priest's son who had not only worked with Coventry Cathedral architect Basil Spence but believed in the liturgical changes coming from the Second Vatican Council. He produced the bold plan to build a new church attached to the ruin rather than rebuild the old one. The unrecognizable All Saints re-opened in 1970.

Relocated in the new church gallery from the tower are two grand memorials. One is to Sir Orlando Gee who, according to the inscription, died in 1705 having served, among others, the Duchess of Somerset who was married in the church.

A tiny octagonal Joshua Chapel, named after a child who died, overlooks the river and has seating in an oval. The sundial outside, a memorial to a Governor-General of Jamaica, shows the time in Jamaica, Jerusalem and Moscow.

The parish embraces Syon House, seat of the Duke of Northumberland, which for a century before the Reformation was the double community of Syon Abbey. There is a brass of Syon nun Margaret Dely in the mansion's Long Room. In 1535 Syon monk Richard Reynolds was hanged at Tyburn alongside the vicar of Isleworth, John Haile. Both had resisted Henry VIII's wish to divorce Katharine of Aragon and today the two martyrs are recognized as St Richard Reynolds and Blessed John Haile. An annual martyrs procession was a feature of village life from 1907 until 1976.

A later vicar, Thomas Hawkes, was visited by William Shakespeare who came up the Thames from Blackfriars and appears to have had relatives here. Leonard Shakespeare, born about 1598, lived until 1664, which was just a year before the bodies of Great Plague victims were brought by barge from the City of London to be buried in a pit behind the church. Later City apprentices, regularly rowing up

Isleworth Church

from London on their annual day off, gave their name to the nearby eighteenth-century Apprentice pub.

In the nineteenth century parishioners included J. M. W. Turner who sketched the church. He lived briefly opposite at the now rebuilt Ferry House which in the second half of the twentieth century was the home of Conservative cabinet minister Lord Gilmour.

At that time Archdeacon Derek Hayward was the incumbent as well as being a City financier and then Secretary of the Diocese of London. He enjoyed commuting by motorbike.

Open on the first Sunday afternoon of the month June to October
Church Street TW7 6BE
www.allsaints-isleworth.org.uk

46
St James, Garlickhythe
Anglican

St James is set beside the fast-flowing traffic in Upper Thames Street and so is best approached down the medieval Garlick Hill where the figure of St James can be seen standing with pilgrim staff in hand on top of the projecting clock.

This is the Apostle James the Great whose tomb at Santiago de Compostela in northern Spain has long drawn pilgrims. Garlickhythe recalls a regular delivery of 'garlick' on the nearby quay but sometimes ships brought back pilgrims from the Galician coast who had visited the shrine.

A church existed here in at least 1170 when it was known as St James apud viniteriam, meaning near Vintry. Later it was called St James apud Tamisyam, meaning near the Thames. Garlickhythe has the oldest set of registers of any parish church and in 1375 its St James Guild operated the earliest form of pension or insurance scheme.

The old church was destroyed in the Great Fire of 1666 and today's building is largely Christopher Wren's design with a tower added by Hawksmoor. The high roof church, known as 'Wren's Lantern', has numerous decorative shells, the symbol of St James, and many seventeenth-century fittings from the now disappeared church called St Michael in Queenhithe. The painting of the Ascension over the altar is by Andrew Geddes whose brother was a curate here.

In World War One a bomb just missed the church and, in thanksgiving, an annual Bomb Sermon was preached for a decade. During World War Two a bomb hit the church, exposing the crypt, but failed to explode. In 1991, shortly after a major refurbishment, a 170-foot crane crashed through the roof between the very same pillars just missed by the bomb. Motorists on the road outside were saved from injury when the traffic lights changed to red seconds before the crane toppled from the Vintners' Place building site opposite.

The Vintners' Company, clutching posies to ward off smells in the narrow lanes, come in procession

The figure of St James on the outside clock

St James, Garlickhythe

every summer for their annual service, bringing a wine porter to walk ahead with a broom clearing a path of any obstructions. Decorative grapes and leaves on the church railing outside were donated by the Vintners.

St James's welcomes a large number of children from London schools as part of its education programme linked to the National Curriculum.

A stamp is kept in a drawer for pilgrims to Santiago who wish to have their credential, or 'pilgrim passport', endorsed as they set out for France and Spain on foot or bicycle.

On Sundays there is a 1662 Prayer Book Sung Eucharist. Eleven livery companies including the Glass Sellers, Horners and Needlemakers are associated with the church and hold services here. The Skinners' Company comes from nearby Dowgate Hill on Corpus Christi in an annual City procession which has taken place since 1393.

Open Monday to Friday 10.30am to 4pm
Garlick Hill EC4V 2AL
www.stjamesgarlickhythe.org.uk

47
St James's, Piccadilly
Anglican

The plain brick church with Portland stone dressings and an outdoor pulpit stands on Piccadilly along from Fortnum & Mason. There is also an entrance on Jermyn Street which was the intended front. Indeed the vestibule under the tower has become a handy walk-through, allowing passers-by a clear view down the wide nave to the Grinling Gibbons' reredos. John Evelyn said that 'there was no altar anywhere in England more handsomely adorned'.

Evelyn was writing in 1684 when the church opened as the final addition to Henry Jermyn's residential development on St James's Fields. The architect was Sir Christopher Wren who had probably been hired by Jermyn when they met in France in 1665. The following year's unexpected Great Fire in the City and planning problems both delayed work. It is the only Wren church to stand on a new site.

The organ was installed in 1691 having been made for James II's Roman Catholic chapel in Whitehall. Henry Purcell, who knew the instrument, came to test it. William Pitt, Prime Minister at the age of 25, and William Blake were both baptized in the superb font made by Grinling Gibbons. The modern east window is by Christopher Webb who included a pelican feeding her young to echo the one in Gibbons' carving below.

In 1940 a World War Two bomb brought down the steeple, severely damaging the church and destroying the rectory. The restoration by Sir Albert Richardson was complete by 1954.

Burials include auctioneer James Christie, who in 1766 founded nearby Christie's, and caricaturist James Gillray. The most unusual wedding was in 1865 when explorer Sir Samuel Baker married a young woman he had bought at a Turkish slave auction.

Four incumbents, including William Temple, have became Archbishop of Canterbury. William Baddeley, brother of actress Hermione, was rector in the 1970s. His successor, Donald Reeves, was largely responsible for shaping the radical agenda for which the church has become so well known. 'On my arrival I could see no justification for keeping the church open,' Reeves recalled. One hotel nearby, offering midnight Mass as part of its Christmas package, asked for an assurance from the new radical rector that there would be no mention of poverty

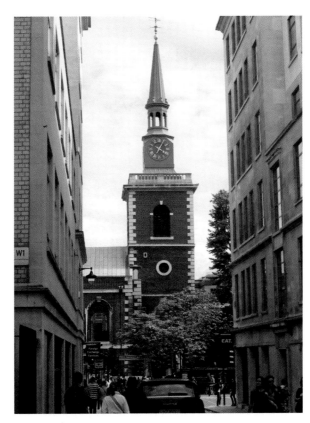

*St James's,
Piccadilly*

in the sermon. Fr Reeves and the congregation were greatly influenced by Bishop Trevor Huddleston who spent his last years at the rectory.

Churchmanship at St James's could be described as very liberal catholic although occasional dance tends to confirm critics' suspicions about a 'New Age' drift. The last rector appeared in an advertisement for alternative power.

The mission statement claims that the congregation 'gathers as a body which welcomes and celebrates human diversity, including spirituality, ethnicity, gender and sexual orientation'. St James's also claims 'to create a space where people of any faith or none can question and discover the sacred life through openness, struggle, laughter and prayer'.

There is a very full talks programme in addition to a lunchtime concert series which has been running for 50 years. The north courtyard hosts a crowded market and the Church Room, added on the south side in 1899, is now a Caffè Nero branch.

Open daily
Piccadilly W1J 9LL
www.st-james-piccadilly.org

48
St James's, Spanish Place
Roman Catholic

The large gothic church is wedged between George Street and Blandford Street near the south end of Marylebone High Street.

The first church was the Spanish Embassy Chapel which from 1791 stood opposite on the corner of George Street and Spanish Place. The embassy occupied Hartford House which is now the Wallace Collection. The chapel's architect was Joseph Bonomi, whose grandson Edward Goldie designed the present church.

The embassy moved in 1827 leaving a viable congregation using a building on a short lease. By the 1880s some £30,000 had been raised for a new building, and when the site opposite came on the market for exactly £30,000 it was snapped up by the priest, Canon William Barry. The new church opened in 1890. King Alfonso XII of Spain contributed to the building fund and later Alfonso XIII and Queen Ena used seats under the two crowns high up in the sanctuary. The Spanish Royal Standard, presented to be flown during royal visits, is above the sacristy door.

The church, with a high roof and 2,000 seats, looks like a cathedral and indeed its George Street entrance is a copy of Lichfield Cathedral's west door. John Francis Bentley decorated many of the chapels including the Lady Chapel, where there is a copy of the *Immaculate Conception* by Murillo. This was the gift of the Count de Torre Díaz. The *Our Lady of Fatima* statue was given in 1949 by the Duchess of Palmella, wife of the Portuguese ambassador.

The church's dedication is to the apostle St James the Great, Spain's patron saint, whose remains are at Santiago de Compostela. His scallop symbol appears throughout the church and his life is told in the windows. A large marble statue of St James depicts him dressed as a pilgrim for the journey to Santiago.

In 1908 Edward VII and Queen Alexandra arrived with a Household Cavalry sovereign's escort for the requiem of King Carlos of Portugal and Prince Luis. Funerals include Russian dancer Vaslav Nijinsky in 1950 and architect Giles Gilbert Scott in 1960.

Novelist Dornford Yates married here in 1919. A decade later Zita James, one of the aristocratic Bright Young People of the 1920s, had her wedding here and remained faithful to the Catholic faith until her death at the age of 102. Vivien Leigh had bridesmaids in peach satin carrying chrysanthemums for her first wedding in 1932. Actor Richard Greene had a wartime wedding in 1940.

St James's, Spanish Place

The gleaming and cared-for feel has been greatly helped by John Paul Getty who gave a generous donation towards restoration after being visited in a clinic by the parish priest.

This is a beautiful church where people drop in to pray during the week. On Sunday there is a very mixed congregation attracted from across London for Mass in English, a Tridentine Mass and a modern Latin Mass, when the choir sings unseen from the gallery.

Open daily
George Street W1U 3QY
www.sjrcc.org.uk

49
St James's, Sussex Gardens
Anglican

This is an important landmark seen from Hyde Park and G. E. Street's last church. According to John Betjeman it is the architect's best. But it is not entirely Street's for he retained the tower from the first church built in 1843. This was by John Goldicutt who had placed the tower and spire at the east end. Street reversed the traditional arrangement and moved the altar to the west end.

The foundation stone for the new gothic church was laid in 1882 by Princess Christian, Queen Victoria's third daughter, just two months after Street's death. The construction work was completed in just a year. The oak pew ends were carved in the building by church members who had to be trained. A slight slope allows at the west end for a crypt which became a shelter during the World War Two Blitz – when the spire was lost and the windows shattered.

Despite war, the church's centenary year was marked in 1943 with £8,000 raised for restoration when peace came. In 1951 the church's west end window was restored to include the image of Bishop James Hannington who preached his farewell sermon here before going to his martyrdom in Uganda. Also depicted is Robert Baden-Powell who was baptized in the first church, and Alexander Fleming who discovered penicillin while working at St Mary's Hospital and was present at the dedication. Another light shows a steam engine leaving Paddington Station. Baden-Powell's godfather was George Stephenson's son Robert.

This early repair took place during the incumbency of George Chappell who was vicar for 30 years from 1941 and oversaw the rebuilding of the hall which incorporated a new vicarage and clergy flats at the west end. Princess Marina, Duchess of Kent, opened the advanced complex in 1958. Seven years later the Paddington Churches Housing Association, which now manages more than 20,000 houses, was founded in the vestry as an answer to Rachmanisn. In this the vicar was assisted by his churchwarden and ecclesiastical lawyer David Faull.

Fr Chappell lived to the age of 101 which was long enough for him to see his own development superseded by today's radical scheme, creating new meeting spaces and dwellings – including another new vicarage. The church interior has been re-ordered with a simple freestanding altar and dramatic lighting.

One of the first couples to marry in the Street church was Oscar Wilde and Constance Lloyd. Others associated with the church include Thora Hird, who

St James's, Sussex Gardens

took charge of the make-up for the pantomime, and actor John Westbrook whose familiar BBC Home Service voice could often be heard reading a lesson.

The parish includes not only Paddington Station and part of Hyde Park but also teeming Queensway. The Eucharist is the centre of worship with a dignified liturgy and challenging preaching. There is an anticipated Sunday Mass on Saturday evening and a professional choir for Sunday's main Eucharist and evensong.

Open daily
Sussex Gardens W2 3UD
www.stjamespaddington.org.uk

50
St John-at-Hampstead
Anglican

This delightful Georgian building stands in the wide Church Row, surrounded by trees and hidden tombs of the famous, and protected by railings and gates from Canons Park (see page 112). The inside of the brick construction has been darkened by both mature trees and Victorian re-ordering.

Hampstead's church is rarely called by its dedication. The old church was referred to as St Mary-in-the-Fields but the eighteenth-century building was called St John's. Which John this referred to was never clear until 1916 when the Bishop of London decided on St John the Evangelist. Both the Baptist and Evangelist are depicted in windows above the altar.

The first church dated from at least the thirteenth century and belonged to Westminster Abbey. When Henry VIII closed the monastery the short-lived Bishop of Westminster was also the rector here.

The present building was erected in 1747 on the site of the medieval church and was viewed soon after by Samuel Johnson. Transepts were added in the 1840s but still it proved too small.

In the 1870s George Gilbert Scott rallied Hampstead against extending the church eastwards. A petition from Holman Hunt, Burne-Jones, Dante Gabriel Rossetti, James Tissot, Anthony Trollope, G. F. Bodley and Norman Shaw resulted in today's arrangement, which has turned the interior round to face west. The architect responsible for this delicate commission was F. P. Cockerell.

In 1952 art historian Kenneth Clark and architectural historian John Summerson headed the roof appeal. In earlier times pew rents produced an income, and the one reserved for the editor of *Punch* still bears its nameplate.

Memorials indicate the high profile over many years of Hampstead residents. The Selwyn brothers, including George, the first Bishop of New Zealand, who gave his name to Selwyn College Cambridge, are recalled in the Lady Chapel. Sir William Woods, Queen Victoria's first Garter King of Arms, has a tablet in the nave, and in the gallery there is the sarcophagus, topped with books, of Longman's founder Thomas Longman.

Keats, who seems to be one of the few famous Hampstead residents not to be buried here, has a bust presented in 1894 by admiring Americans. In the church-yard are the tombs of artist John Constable and marine chronometer inventor

St John-at-Hampstead

John Harrison. The churchyard extension, which runs up Holly Hill almost to St Mary's, holds historian Walter Besant, early TV personality Professor Joad, actress Kay Kendall, Labour leader Hugh Gaitskell, Home Secretary Frank Soskice, and Eleanor Farjeon who wrote the hymn 'Morning has broken'.

More recent funerals include Peter Cook in 1995 whose death brought his colleague Dudley Moore to the church for one of his last public appearances. Weddings have included poet Coventry Patmore in 1847 and actor Paul Nicholls in 2008.

The congregation was recently described as 'large, vibrant and intellectually curious'. Its future looks secure with five Sunday school groups. There is weekly Choral Evensong. Also based here with on-site productions are the Hampstead Players.

Open daily
Church Row NW3 6UU
www.hampsteadparishchurch.org.uk

51
St John's, Downshire Hill
Anglican

The simple white stucco church with a cupola looks as if it should be in America, as do some of the equally charming whitewashed houses around it. The interior is just as plain with a double staircase in the entrance leading to a gallery and a simple altar below a reredos displaying the Ten Commandments, the Lord's Prayer and the Apostles' Creed.

John Betjeman knew the chapel from childhood and described it as 'remarkable' and deserving to be cherished. It is the only proprietary chapel within the London Diocese. The builder was Downshire Hill developer William Woods from Kennington who completed the building over five years in-between work on the houses. The project was supported by the Reverend James Curry and lawyer Edward Carlisle with the first service held in 1823.

John Keats, who lived across the road on the south side, watched the beginning of building work in 1818 and 1819. The first chaplain, William Harness, was a friend of Byron.

The clock is as old as the church and will have been seen over the years by such residents as Bernard Shaw, D. H. Lawrence, Stanley Spencer, Katherine Mansfield, Flora Robson and Edith Sitwell.

Although William Harness was described as high church this did not mean that he was catholic. The chapel has an evangelical tradition and its independence from the parish annoyed the long-standing rector of Hampstead Samuel White, who in 1832 managed to get the chapel closed for three years despite a petition signed by Samuel Taylor Coleridge's daughter Sara. Keats described the rector, whose father purchased the living for him, as 'the parson of Hampstead quarrelling with all the world'.

The east window, the only stained glass one, was added in 1882 and some restoration was undertaken in 1896. More improvements were made in the 1960s by architect Edward Cullinan who added the west end's glass screens.

Shortly afterwards Bishop Kenneth Howell became chaplain to the small congregation. However, when he left, the post remained vacant for more than two years and numbers attending dwindled. Only after a new appointment in 1981 was there some growth, which was fortunate as the lack of proper foundations meant that urgent repair work could not be delayed indefinitely. In 2003 a stronger

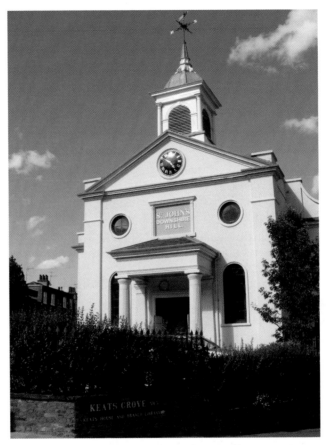

St John's, Downshire Hill

congregation, which had continued renting the church for a pound a year from a family trust, purchased the building and began a major restoration programme. A £2.5 million scheme has not only underpinned the building, but created an undercroft that is rented out for parties and functions to create an income.

Meanwhile, in the church, the original box pews with umbrella racks remain at the sides although chairs are now the main seating for services and occasional concerts.

The church, which maintains its evangelical tradition, runs Bible study groups, a free weekly parents and toddlers group called Mini Mischief, an after-school club, and a youth group called Aliens.

The church can be viewed through glass inner doors daily
Downshire Hill NW3 1NU
www.sjdh.org

52

St John's, Stratford Broadway

Anglican

Stratford town centre is dominated by its church whose very high spire can be seen far away. With its large clock, St John's stands like an ancient town church, providing an important focus in a busy market packed with shoppers and a main road with constant traffic heading into London from Essex.

The pews are dark wood but the plain glass in the windows, a result of wartime bombing, makes the church light.

St John's dates only from 1834 when the vicar of West Ham realized that tiny Stratford was growing. This was before the arrival of the railway. The land was given by the Duke of Wellington's brother, Lord Wellesley-Pole of Wanstead.

The architect was Edward Blore who imposed the Early English style. The interior is the result of major changes in the 1880s when a gallery was removed. Enlarging the chancel involved cutting the carved Caen stone reredos in half and placing sections on either side. A plaque records that this was done in memory of the naturalist and church reformer Sir Antonio Brady who is buried in the churchyard.

By this time it had become a separate parish from West Ham. During World War Two, when many used the crypt as a shelter, the church was badly damaged by bombing.

Restoration was finished in 1951. Forty-five years later a carefully designed extension was added to the north side by Purcell Miller Tritton, the architects associated with the restorations at Christ Church in Spitalfields and St Ethelburga's in Bishopsgate. It is hardly discernible from a distance but provides a multi-use community facility which also allows for the church itself to now be open daily. It is St John's contribution to the regeneration of Stratford.

The prominent six-sided Martyrs Memorial opposite the west end was added in 1879 to commemorate the 23 local male and female Protestant martyrs burnt at the stake in 1556 during the reign of Mary I.

The church retains an evangelical ministry although two assistant clergy became leading Anglo-Catholics. A curate in 1883–5 was Arthur Durrant who began the catholic tradition at Holy Trinity, Leverstock Green in Hertfordshire, while vicar there for 36 years. Frank Weston, the future curate of St Matthew's in Westminster and Bishop of Zanzibar, was deacon at Holy Trinity Mission Church in Oxford

St John's, Stratford Broadway

Road for three years. The vicar at the time was Thomas Stevens who became the first Bishop of Barking in 1901.

Former parishioners include priest and poet Gerard Manley Hopkins who was baptized here in 1844. Earlier his family, living in The Grove opposite, had contributed to the building fund.

The parish runs west as far as the River Lea on the edge of Bow and includes both the Three Mills film studios and most of the Olympic park. The population is very mixed with many immigrants, including recent arrivals from Eastern Europe. In the 1970s the congregation was small but now an average Sunday morning attendance is well over 200.

Open daily
Broadway E15 1NG
www.stjohnse15.co.uk

53
St John's, Waterloo
Anglican

The classical church, now sometimes known as St John's-by-the-IMAX, is best seen from a train passing from Charing Cross and Waterloo East. The nave is exceptionally wide.

St John's was designed by Francis Bedford and built in 1824 as one of the 'Waterloo Churches' funded as a thanksgiving for the end of hostilities with the French.

One of the first organists was Charles Wesley's grandson Samuel Sebastian Wesley. Felix Mendelssohn played the much acclaimed instrument, which survives. The organ's power was reduced as a result of wartime bombing in 1940 which left the church roofless.

St John's re-opened in 1951 as the Festival of Britain Church after Sybil Thorndike, based at the nearby Old Vic, had helped to raise money. Hans Feibusch provided the east end paintings. The paschal candlestick is Royal Doulton. The Festival Bible is on display.

The Festival legacy is the Royal Festival Hall and the clergy are chaplains to the National Theatre, the Old Vic, Young Vic and London Television Centre studios. When the Young Vic had to close for rebuilding it brought its community opera to the church. Other productions staged here include *Murder in the Cathedral*.

Kristin Scott Thomas is patron of the Voice Factory in the crypt which provides tuition for actors and singers. Also here is Southbank Mosaics. Other initiatives born out of St John's are the South Bank Christian Studies Centre and St Andrew's, a new church off The Cut.

In 1889 the Princess of Wales attended one of the monthly organ recitals with choir and orchestra. Now there are free 'Rush Hour Concerts' with wine in the late afternoon, provided by the Southbank Sinfonia founded by the church to launch new musicians.

Behind St John's is the nineteenth-century Roupell Street which represents how the area looked when Waterloo was a small station and the South Bank was occupied by the Lion Brewery. In the mid-1970s the population dropped so much that two schools closed. However, in the last decade of the twentieth century the population doubled.

The church has a youth club, a girls' football team and a Godly Play Room for

St John's, Waterloo

toddlers. The large church is a popular venue not just for concerts and exhibitions but national church conferences and the diocesan synod. The north wall is covered by a tapestry to which almost every Southwark Diocese parish contributed.

Among recent rectors is John Ford, whose daughter Anna became ITV's first female newsreader. Canon Richard Truss, featured in a book by controversial Bishop Jack Spong who spoke here, recruited curates by describing Waterloo as 'the most interesting parish in the country'.

Both George Carey and his successor Rowan Williams have come from nearby Lambeth Palace to celebrate the Eucharist. Princess Alexandra visited in 2001 to mark the 50th anniversary of the Festival of Britain.

The congregation includes many residents involved in trying to shape the regeneration of the parish, which includes both the riverside with the London Eye and also social housing.

Open daily
Waterloo Road SE1 8TY
www.stjohnswaterloo.co.uk

54

St Katharine's Danish Church, Regent's Park

Lutheran

The high stone west front resembles the chapel of King's College Cambridge and its twin spires are reminiscent of those of Cologne Cathedral when seen rising above the sunken mews houses to the north.

St Katharine's, designed by young architect Ambrose Poynter, was built in 1826–8 for the Royal Foundation of St Katharine whose ancient riverside site to the east of the Tower of London was being dug out to create St Katharine Dock. The chapel, dating from 1340, was demolished.

St Katharine's Hospital had been founded in 1147 by Queen Matilda, wife of King Stephen. Her successor Queen Eleanor, widow of Henry III, refounded it as a religious community with a hospital and school under the patronage of the Queens of England.

It is remarkable for having escaped closure during the dissolution of the monasteries. Indeed Katharine of Aragon remained patron after her divorce from Henry VIII, and the Master of St Katharine's presided at her funeral.

In 1948, when the Foundation moved to the East End, the Regent's Park buildings were made available to the Danish Church.

The Foundation took with it the remaining fourteenth-century stalls rescued from the original site so the church's east end interior now appears minimalist with a modern altar, pulpit and font. But above the altar is a large 1887 window with strong colours and many figures.

Under the high nave windows are the shields of the patrons from founder Queen Matilda to Queen Mary (1926–53). At the back of the church there is the Danish royal coat of arms.

Also at the west end are the carved figures of Moses and John the Baptist brought from the former Danish Church at Limehouse. They are the work of Danish sculptor Caius Cibber who enjoyed success in England and was appointed Carver to the King's Closet by William III.

In one of the two walled gardens is a copy of the Rune stone set up at Jelling by Harold Bluetooth, the first Christian King of Denmark.

To the east, with a magnificent view of the church, is Park Village West where in

St Katharine's Danish Church, Regent's Park

1845 Dr Edward Pusey founded the first Anglican sisterhood. The house is marked with a plaque.

The Foundation motto is 'Worship, Hospitality and Service' which could also be applied to the Danish Church, which welcomes visiting Danes to meals in a dining room along the north side.

Annual events include the Lucia service in December which is followed by traditional doughnuts and glögg. This Swedish custom spread to Denmark at the end of World War Two as a mark of resistance to the Nazis.

A model sailing ship is suspended at the west end, symbolizing the church's mission to Danish sailors in the ports of London and Shoreham in Sussex.

Open Tuesday to Friday 9am to 1pm; weekends noon to 5pm
Outer Circle, Regent's Park NW1 4HH
www.danskekirke.org

55
Kingston Parish Church, Kingston upon Thames
Anglican

The church has a distinctive new tower echoing the Guildhall. From Thames Street it is possible to look down an alley and directly into the nave. But the best entry is through the market and churchyard on the south side.

The tower was built in 1979 but there are older stones below. One is a Saxon fragment that may date from the Great Council held in 838 by King Egbert. Six Saxon kings were crowned at Kingston so it is assumed that there was a church here. The present one was begun in 1120 and the four tower pillars are thirteenth century. The small painting of St Blaise on a south transept pillar is fourteenth century. He is patron of wool merchants and a reminder of Kingston's medieval trade. Holy Trinity Chapel, built in 1477 by the Shipman's Guild, a branch of the Corporation of Trinity House now responsible for lighthouses, is an indication of the town's port status.

A frequent traveller by water to Kingston upon Thames would have been the Bishop of Winchester who had a house on the Bishop Out of Residence pub site where he could rest before continuing to his Southwark residence downstream. Kingston was within the vast Winchester Diocese until the nineteenth century.

The font is probably by Sir Christopher Wren. Nearby is a brass from the tomb of Robert and Joanna Skerne who was Edward III's daughter. Memorials include one to John Heyton who died in 1584 having been Sergeant of the Larder to Queen Mary and Queen Elizabeth. The statue of a seated Countess of Liverpool, wife of George IV's Prime Minister who lived at New Malden, is a rare freestanding figure by Sir Francis Chantry.

Incumbents include Patrick Magee who had been a King's College Cambridge chorister and sang a solo during the first Christmas Eve broadcast of *Nine Lessons and Carols* in 1928. However, in Kingston during the 1950s, he was better known as an accomplished mimic who dressed as a woman to open the parish bazaar.

This is the setting for Sir John Millais' 'Sermon' paintings showing a young girl awake and then asleep in a high back pew. Chairs replaced pews in 1979 when the church was re-ordered and the altar placed beneath the tower. This appeared

Kingston Parish Church, Kingston upon Thames

revolutionary at the time but the altar is now recognized as being on the probable site of the church's Saxon east end.

All Saints is a flourishing town centre church with a new logo and expansion plans. It has a strong musical tradition with both a men's choir and a girls' choir which combine on major feasts. Evensong is sung every Sunday and choirs from home and abroad visit. The new Danish Frobenius organ is specially designed for use in worship, orchestral concerts and recitals.

Volunteer vergers keep the church open every day. Sundays are considered important not only for services but for shoppers who may drop in, making contact with the church for the first time.

Open daily
The Market Place KT1 1JP
www.allsaintskingston.co.uk

56

St Lawrence Whitchurch, Little Stanmore

Anglican

The church is found in a gap in a long suburban street. Suddenly there is grass and a church beyond a lychgate. Walking into the building is like entering a stately home. 'St Lawrence is not just one of the churches of Middlesex, it has one of the most splendid Georgian interiors in England,' observed John Betjeman.

The parish church was rebuilt in 1715 as an indulgence by James Brydges, later Duke of Chandos, who had bought Canons Park. The name refers to the canons of St Bartholomew's Priory in Smithfield who orginally held the land. Whitchurch comes from Whyte Churche, meaning white church.

The church architect was John James who also worked on the rebuilding of the Duke's house. He kept the medieval tower but attached an outstanding example of a continental baroque eighteenth-century church. It has the feel of a family chapel and was used as such until the chapel in the house was completed in 1720. In the church there is just a central aisle for accessing the box pews which all have doors. The Duke's pew is high up at the west end where he sat under a copy of Raphael's *Transfiguration* found at the Vatican.

The vaulted ceiling has paintings of Christ's miracles and teachings painted by Louis Laguerre whose other work is at Chatsworth and Blenheim. The altar is flanked by Gaetano Brunnetti's *Adoration of the Shepherds* and *The Descent from the Cross.*

Behind the altar is an open stage with proscenium arch by Grinling Gibbons. Handel, the Duke's composer in residence, played the organ; this has a Gibbons' casing and is centrally placed so it can be surrounded by an orchestra. Here Handel composed two settings of the Te Deum, 12 Chandos Anthems and the hymn tune 'Cannons' for his friends John and Charles Wesley. Part of Handel's *Suite des Pieces pour le Clavecine* is known as 'The Harmonious Blacksmith' as its rhythm is said to have been inspired by the parish clerk William Powell hammering in his smithy. The grave of the 'Harmonious Blacksmith' is in the churchyard.

Attached to the church is the Chandos Mausoleum where the Duke can be seen in huge effigy dressed as a Roman with two of his three wives kneeling on each side. This was all completed long before his death in 1789.

St Lawrence Whitchurch, Little Stanmore

The only modern additions to the church are a freestanding altar, which easily fits, and a Lady Chapel created in 1966 at the base of the tower.

Canons has gone but the name was taken by the Underground station. A causeway used by the Duke to reach his church is discernible in the now public park's sweeping grass.

The church maintains a catholic tradition in sympathy with its decoration although there is no incense in deference to the precious paintings. The congregation is drawn from the residential roads built on the Duke's former estate.

Open Sunday 2pm to 4pm; summer 2pm to 5pm
Whitchurch Lane HA8 6RB
www.little-stanmore.org

57
London Oratory, Brompton Road
Roman Catholic

The Oratory has been described as a baroque church plucked up from the Roman corso and dropped in west London next to the Victoria & Albert Museum. The church interior, with Venetian mosaics below the dome, has a nave wider than St Paul's Cathedral.

The London Oratory is the church of a priest community known as the Congregation of the Oratory of St Philip Neri. Cardinal Henry Newman knew the mother house in Rome and founded England's Oratories at Birmingham, where he lived, and Brompton. Since Newman was assisted by former Anglican Fr Frederick Faber, who became the first London superior, it can be said that the Oratory is the fruit of the Oxford Movement.

When the site in Brompton Road was chosen in 1852 there was concern that it was too far outside London. The architect Herbert Gribble was chosen for the task by Alfred Waterhouse who was working on designs for his huge Prudential building in Holborn. Enough of the church was finished by 1884 for Cardinal Henry Manning to be able to preside at the opening. The church is dedicated to the Immaculate Heart of Our Blessed Lady.

Gribble suggested that those who had no opportunity of going to Italy to see an Italian church had only to come here and for a time the Oratory even observed the Roman custom by closing in the early afternoon. The interior became even more Italian over the following 15 years with statues of the apostles, which had lined Siena Cathedral, being added along with a seventeenth-century Lady Chapel altar from Brescia.

The altar of St Philip Neri was donated by the fourteenth Duke of Norfolk after a chance meeting with Fr Faber. The vested wax effigy of the saint adds to the Italian feel.

The grotto-like St Wilfred's Chapel in the far south-east corner contains Rex Whistler's only religious work, which is a triptych of St Thomas More and St John Fisher commissioned to mark their canonization in 1938.

Weddings have included those of composer Edward Elgar in 1889 and film director Alfred Hitchcock in 1936. John F. Kennedy worshipped here as a child.

The Oratory managed to interpret the late twentieth-century changes to the liturgy with such skill that only minimum alterations needed to be made to the

London Oratory, Brompton Road

main Masses which continue to be celebrated in Latin. The choir is noted for its plainchant and performances of traditional Mass settings at Sunday's Solemn Mass when the church is packed by people of all ages. The congregation retains that slight suggestion that a number of its regular members may be, as they are, from 'Old Catholic families'.

At Christmas there is an orchestra and on Good Friday and Holy Saturday it is still possible to attend Tenebrae. Hymns occasionally sung include of course Newman's 'Lead kindly light' and Faber's 'Faith of our fathers'.

Appropriately, Cardinal Newman's statue welcomes visitors approaching the church from Brompton Road.

Open daily 7am to 6pm (Sunday 7pm)
Brompton Road SW7 2RP
www.bromptonoratory.com

58

St Magnus the Martyr, Lower Thames Street

Anglican

This Wren church is by the Thames and at the bottom of Fish Street Hill below The Monument. Drivers in Lower Thames Street might hardly notice it as its north side by the road is a high blank wall with blocked-up windows. The windows were filled in as early as 1782 when traffic noise first invaded the church.

The 1234 building, mentioned by Shakespeare in *Henry VI Part II*, was the second church to be consumed by the Great Fire in 1666. At that time London Bridge was nearer the church and in 1759 the river crossing was made so wide that the downstream pavement ran through the base of the tower, which features in two of Claude Monet's river paintings.

The church was described by John Betjeman as 'Wren's welcome to the City for people coming over Old London Bridge' but in 1832 the bridge was rebuilt a little further upstream which robbed St Magnus of its commanding position at the entrance to the City. The now partly hidden clock was donated in 1709 by a Lord Mayor, Sir George Duncombe, who, as a young apprentice from Southwark across the river, had been in trouble for arriving late for work. He also gave the organ.

The church interior was re-ordered in 1925 by Martin Travers and gives the impression that the Reformation never happened. It was described by T. S. Eliot as 'inexplicable splendour of Ionian white and gold' at the time when outside there was a strong smell of fish from the nearby Billingsgate Market. Indeed for a time the fish harvest festival was held here.

Rector and Bible translator Miles Coverdale is buried in the church. An influential twentieth-century rector, from 1922 until 1959, was Henry Fynes-Clinton who was both a leading Anglo-Catholic and a campaigner for Christian Unity. He was a friend of Spencer Jones who co-founded the Week of Prayer for Christian Unity and was invited to preach here every January. Fr Fynes-Clinton was responsible for bringing Abbé Courturier and Spencer Jones together and widening the idea of unity embracing not just the Anglican and Roman Catholic Churches but also the Orthodox and Protestant churches.

Fr Fynes-Clinton was the first City incumbent to introduce lunchtime services.

St Magnus the Martyr, Lower Thames Street

He also refounded the Fraternity of Our Lady of Salve Regina which was originally a devotional guild for fishmongers. At his funeral, Billingsgate porters, holding their traditional hats, lined the street.

An attraction is a large model of London Bridge complete with houses and chapel made by David Aggett.

With the Friends of the City Churches office based in the rectory, this church, with a daily Mass, is a focus for activity and outreach. Every year on Baptism Sunday the congregation joins the Southwark Cathedral congregation on London Bridge for the Orthodox custom of blessing the river.

Open Tuesday to Friday 10am to 4pm
Lower Thames Street EC3R 6DN
www.stmagnusmartyr.org.uk

59

St Margaret's, Westminster

Anglican

St Margaret's, which is older than it looks from the outside, is the little church alongside Westminster Abbey.

The first church here was built in about 1120 for the local residents who were not part of the Abbey's monastic community. The present building was consecrated in 1523 and encased in Portland stone 200 years later.

The interior is clearly a Tudor church although the east window, made in about 1523 to mark the wedding of Henry VIII and Katharine of Aragon, was not installed until 1758. Buried below in front of the altar is Sir Walter Raleigh.

A window honours parishioner John Milton who is seen meeting Galileo in Florence. War-damaged windows have been filled with John Piper glass but a fragment of saved glass shows William Caxton demonstrating his printing press which was located close to here.

There is a memorial to panorama engraver Wenceslaus Hollar who is buried in an unmarked grave in the now grassed churchyard.

Above the small east porch is a bust of Charles I placed there soon after the large statue of Oliver Cromwell was allowed outside Parliament opposite in 1899. In the spacious front porch, added in 1891 to a design by J. L. Pearson, is a memorial to the popular preacher William Farrar who was rector in the late nineteenth century. His children's book *Eric or Little by Little* was a bestseller.

Among the organists are the organ builder Bernard 'Father' Smith, from 1676 to 1708, who was soon followed by Edward Purcell, son of the composer.

Weddings here include those of Samuel Pepys and Winston Churchill. On show is Churchill's application to be on the parish electoral roll signed as a resident at 11 Downing Street. The choir sang at number 10 when Edward Heath was Prime Minister. Although this ceased to be a parish church in 1973, when it was returned to the care of the Abbey, it is still best known as 'the parish church of the House of Commons'.

This association began in 1614 and the rector, as Speaker's Chaplain, leads prayers in the Commons' chamber at the start of each day's sitting. At St Margaret's there is a pew for Mr Speaker and the kneelers are decorated with the Commons' crowned portcullis symbol. The pulpit was given in memory of Thomas Vacher, founder of *Vacher's Parliamentary Companion*. Also commemorated

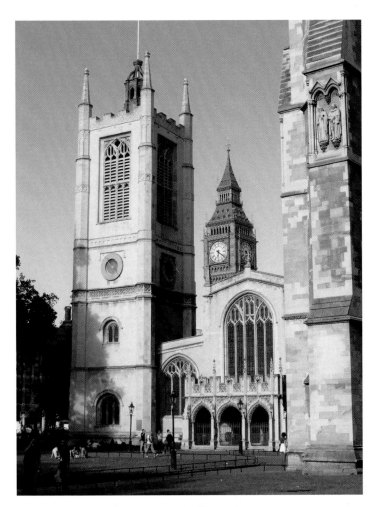

St Margaret's, Westminster

here is his contemporary Thomas Erskine May, who wrote the standard guide to parliamentary procedure.

Both Lloyd George and Churchill led MPs from the Commons to the church at the conclusion of both world wars.

This church is the venue for politicians' memorial services and the Parliamentary Carol Service. The bells peal out on special occasions such as the State Opening of Parliament.

Open daily
Parliament Square SW1P 3JX
www.westminster-abbey.org/st-margarets

60
St Martin's, Ruislip
Anglican

This church with its flint and stone dressing tower is found behind timber-framed houses in the High Street where a lychgate leads to a close-like churchyard.

The dedication to St Martin was chosen by the Benedictine Abbey of Bec in Normandy which was granted the manor of Ruislip in 1087 following the Norman invasion. The nearby farm, duck pond and England's oldest barn belonged to the monks who built the church.

The thirteenth-century pillars are the oldest part of the building although the font is twelfth-century Purbeck stone. The chancel, Lady Chapel and tower were rebuilt in 1500. Unusual for the area are the pre-Reformation wall paintings in the nave.

A 1697 charity bread shelf is decorated with a coat of arms belonging to the son of vicar Thomas Bright who rose to be Master of the Leathersellers in the City. Jeremiah Bright provided for two shillings' worth of bread to be distributed to the poor every Sunday and fresh loaves continued to be placed there until 1955.

An unexpected monument for a Middlesex church belongs to Mary Bankes of Corfe in Dorset who held out in its castle against the Roundheads for three years. Her son Ralph included the declaration that she 'had the honour to have born with a constancy and courage above her sex, a noble proportion of the late calamities, and the happiness to have outlived them'. Her father Ralph Hawtrey and his wife, who lived at nearby Eastcote, also have a memorial.

Glass in the fourteenth-century west window includes the shield of King's College Cambridge which succeeded Bec as the manor owner and the shield of St George's Chapel Windsor which has been the church's patron since 1451.

In recent years there have been subtle improvements. The base of the tower is glazed to provide a room for babies and toddlers during services. The pulpit has been turned and the font repositioned. Glass inner doors allow the interior to be seen even when the church is locked.

The large churchyard contains the grave of singer Elisabeth Schumann and a wall plaque to actress Jessie Matthews.

Activities include maintaining the tower clock which has been manually wound since 1886 and running The Priory Bookshop in a Tudor building which has a large upstairs and sells cards, the latest religious books and also secondhand books.

St Martin's, Ruislip

The River Pinn flows across the parish which embraces not only suburban streets but also Ruislip Lido and Mad Bess Wood. St Martin's is so far from central London that it is twinned with the poorer parish of St Michael's in Camden Town.

'Church life extends beyond worship on a Sunday' claims the welcome leaflet. At Ruislip, shoppers drop in to genuflect before the Blessed Sacrament and say a prayer. There is morning prayer, Mass and evening prayer daily. It is one of the few Anglican churches to have an anticipated Sunday Mass on Saturday evening. On Sundays music is provided by a choir, singers and a folk group.

Open daily 8.30am to 4pm
High Street HA4 8DG
www.smartins-ruislip.org

61

St Martin-in-the Fields, Trafalgar Square

Anglican

The church is best seen from the piazza in front of the National Gallery. The nave is light and simple but one's eyes are drawn to an extraordinary window beyond the altar by Iranian artist Shirazeh Houshiary who has produced an eliptical cross likened to the veil of St Veronica touching the face of Jesus.

In the thirteenth century this was a daughter church of Westminster Abbey adjacent to its 'Convent Garden'. Today's building is by James Gibbs and was completed in 1721. The full beauty of the church was not revealed until more than a century later when the area was cleared for Trafalgar Square. But still the spire was 80 feet higher than Nelson. By then the church had been much copied, with St Paul's Chapel in New York's Manhattan being the most famous example.

John Betjeman, who described St Martin's as 'an architectural triumph', observed that the 'steeple seems to ride the portico as though it were on horseback'.

The royal pew, like a box in a theatre, is a reminder that this is the Royal Parish Church. The boundary embraces not Buckingham Palace, which did not exist in the 1720s, but St James's Palace. George I, who had been crowned by the former vicar Thomas Tenison, became churchwarden. Prince Charles was patron of the recent £36 million appeal.

James Oglethorpe, founder of Georgia in the USA, was one of the last to be baptized in the old Tudor church. Painter Benjamin West was married in the present church in 1765 around the time Handel tried out the organ.

This is now a church for memorial services. Some are naval as the Admiralty is also in the parish and has a grand pew. In 1983 the actor Richard Burton's service was attended by three of his wives with the readings delivered by Paul Scofield and John Gielgud. In the same year Bernard Levin gave the address at Rebecca West's service.

Today's outreach ministry began with Dick Sheppard who was vicar in 1914 and opened the doors to troops arriving on boat trains at Charing Cross. In 1924 he agreed to the first broadcast church service. In 1950 the church hosted the first televised Christmas Day service. Today BBC Radio 4 broadcasts from St Martin's every year on Ascension Day.

St Martin-in-the Fields, Trafalgar Square

It was here in 1961 that the idea of Amnesty International was conceived when Peter Benenson dropped in, having read that morning about two students being arrested by Portugal's Salazar regime.

'St Martin-in-the-Fields exists to honour God and enable questioning, open-minded people to discover for themselves the significance of Jesus Christ' says the mission statement. The vicar speaks of the church offering 'practical Christianity'. Its pioneer social care unit sees 7,000 homeless people each year.

The recently expanded crypt is like an Underground station and houses a Les Routiers approved cafe, a shop and a reception desk selling tickets for candlelit concerts. On Sunday two of the five services are in Mandarin and Cantonese.

Open daily
Trafalgar Square WC2N 4JJ
www.stmartin-in-the-fields.org

62

St Mary Abbots, Kensington High Street

Anglican

A cloister-style arcade leads beneath London's tallest spire into a lofty church 179 feet long with seating for 700.

Abbots is derived from the Abbot of Abingdon who founded the church in about 1100 when Kensington was 'near' London. During the 1860s a much rebuilt small church had become inadequate and architect George Gilbert Scott was asked to create an 'exceedingly magnifical' new church.

He responded by declaring the site 'hardly to be surpassed for convenience and grandeur of position' and produced a design that he declared had 'a degree of dignity proportioned to the rank and position of the parish for which it is intended'.

The steeple is a copy of Bristol's St Mary Redcliffe and stands on a tower with an unusual ring of ten bells including some from the old church.

The altar and reredos are Gilbert Scott's design but were completed under his grandson Giles. Two flanking mosaics are by the Salviati workshop in Venice.

On a grey day the church can seem dark but on a sunny day the many richly coloured stained glass windows glow. Forty-eight clerestory windows depict prophets and saints.

Many monuments come from the two previous churches on the site. Commemorated on a choir stall is Henry Curtis who sang in the choir for 80 years until 1965. Another recent plaque honours Christopher Ironside who designed Britain's first decimal coins.

Archbishop of York John Habgood was a curate here in the 1950s. Recent vicar Tim Thornton became Bishop of Sherborne and then Truro. Mr Speaker Onslow was baptized here in 1691. Weddings include magistrate John Fielding in 1774. Broadcaster Nick Clarke had a crowded funeral in 2006.

There is a carpeted royal pew for the residents of Kensington Palace which is in the parish. William and Mary worshipped here and gave the hexagonal pulpit. Princess Louise, Queen Victoria's daughter, came when the congregation was so packed that matins and evensong were both sung twice on a Sunday. Being a sculptor she made the life-size angel memorial to her brothers Alfred and Leopold.

St Mary Abbots, Kensington High Street

Princess Alice, Victoria's last living granddaughter, was still attending in the late 1970s.

As the coffin of Diana, Princess of Wales, left the Palace in 1997 it was the bell of St Mary Abbots that could be heard tolling.

Also within the parish are the *Daily Mail* offices and Heythrop College. This means that, with the addition of a popular church school, the congregation is a mixture of young and old, some with two homes and many in influential occupations. This is the Royal Borough's civic church with a thriving Friends of St Mary Abbots attracting huge local support from business and residents. There are regular concerts by Royal College of Music students.

Both the church's voluntary and professional choirs share the three main Sunday services, which include evensong.

Within the churchyard is the primary school building, forming one side of a wide cathedral-like approach to the west door.

Open daily
Kensington High Street w8 4sp
www.stmaryabbotschurch.org

63

St Mary's, Addington

Anglican

Just ten minutes on a fast tram from Croydon, St Mary's looks like a typical village church. It is opposite The Cricketers pub, named after a cricket club older than the MCC, and alongside an eighteenth-century cottage. The inside of the tiny 900-year-old church has some surprising decoration and monuments.

There has been a church here since 1080 and the present building has a twelfth-century chancel complete with original windows. A brass to John Leigh in the floor dates from the year of Henry VIII's accession. The thirteenth-century south aisle was once thatched.

But what makes this church extra special is its close association with most nineteenth-century Archbishops of Canterbury. After the ancient archbishop's palace in nearby Croydon had been sold in 1780 it was decided that a replacement was needed. Addington Place, once home of the Leigh family, who are much commemorated in the church, was chosen and renamed Addington Palace. From 1805 to 1897 this was the primate's country home. In the 1780s the mansion had been rebuilt by architect Robert Mylne (who had proved himself with the first Blackfriars Bridge) for Lord Mayor of London Sir Barlow Trecothick who is buried in the church. The author and wit Sydney Smith called his extravagant monument 'the Addington pickle jar'. After World War Two the house was occupied by the Royal School of Church Music.

John and Joane Leigh, 1576

The cross in the churchyard was erected in 1911 by Archbishop Randall Davidson in memory of all his predecessors who, unlike him, had lived here. Indeed five are buried in the churchyard, and Davidson, as son-in-law of the last one, Tait, also knew Addington well.

Archbishop Charles Manners-Sutton is buried in the church and his son, who was Speaker of the House of Commons, is commemorated behind the pulpit. Archbishop William Howley, who crowned Queen Victoria, is buried in the chancel. He added

St Mary's, Addington

the porch which has the unfortunate initials 'WC' over the door, derived from his signature 'William Cantuar'.

Archbishops Howley, Sumner and Longley are buried in modest graves in the churchyard. The latter died at Addington Palace in 1868, where he had come to recuperate after suffering from bronchitis, just a year after presiding at the first Lambeth Conference.

The highly decorated east end with its marble reredos is a memorial to Archbishop Edward Benson. It is thanks to him that St Mary's was the first parish church to hold a Nine Lessons and Carols service. The Archbishop had been Bishop of Truro, where he introduced the service in the cathedral on Christmas Eve to counter drunkenness in pubs.

A contemporary was Sir George Johnson, Queen Victoria's doctor, who is commemorated with a window.

Every Sunday morning the bells, one dating from 1390, ring out for a Eucharist. There is a Sunday school, a lively youth club and a branch of the Mothers' Union.

Open May to September on the 2nd and 4th Sunday of the month 2.30pm to 6pm
Addington Village Road CRO 5AS
www.addington.org.uk

64

St Mary-at-Hill, Lovat Lane

Anglican

The church is in the medieval network of narrow hillside lanes, but with its front door in Lovat Lane just visible from Eastcheap. It could be a church in Italy and the exterior gives no clue of the fire damage it has suffered within.

There was a church here in 1177 when the house on the south side became the London home of the new Abbot of Waltham. The abbey in Essex was founded that year as part of Henry II's penance for the murder of Thomas Becket in 1170. The rectory now covers the site of the Abbot's house where a tunnel leads to the east side.

The church was rebuilt in the early sixteenth century when it had a choir of lay clerks and boys, including Thomas Tallis, singing daily services. The tower survived the Great Fire which started in nearby Pudding Lane, and being only partly damaged it was one of the first to be repaired by Wren.

In 1894 it just avoided demolition to make way for the Underground, although 3,000 bodies were removed from the crypt.

In the twentieth century John Betjeman described the church as having 'the least spoiled and most gorgeous interior in the City'. However, in 1988 a fire that went through the roof destroyed many of the fittings. Now where there was a giant wooden reredos there is a curtain, and where box pews once corralled the congregation there are now scattered chairs.

There is an extraordinary new beauty but some of the pews in storage may one day return to allow a hint of how the church looked for 300 years. The 1848 organ, the largest working survivor of one by William Hill, has been rebuilt since the fire.

Rectors have included Church Army founder Wilson Carlisle who served from 1892 to 1926 and Brian Kirk-Duncan, honorary Archdeacon in Guinea, who was here for 44 years from 1962 until his death in 2006.

The Society of Fellowship Porters, dissolved by the Corporation of London at the end of the Victorian era, had an annual service here on the Sunday after St John the Baptist's Day. Charles Dickens may have been inspired by them to create the fictional Six Jolly Fellowship Porters pub in *Our Mutual Friend*.

Today's noted annual service remains the Fish Harvest Festival in October. This is a legacy of when Billingsgate Market at the bottom of the hill was the

St Mary-at-Hill, Lovat Lane

capital's fish market. Until 1982 the smell of fresh fish would waft up Lovat Lane to mingle with the aroma of fresh ground coffee in the warehouses of St Botolph Alley opposite. Dr Kirk-Duncan suggested that the service ought to be held in Docklands where new Billingsgate Market is located but those involved in creating the annual display of fish in the church entrance wanted to retain the connection.

The regular weekly service is a lunchtime Eucharist on Wednesday. There are lunchtime recitals every Thursday.

Open Monday to Friday
Lovat Lane EC3R 8EE
www.stmary-at-hill.org

65
St Mary's, Bourne Street
Anglican

The entrance to the church is a narrow passage between houses. The inside is a breathtaking Anglo-Catholic shrine likened to a grand private house.

This is extraordinary for when the church was built in 1874, over the rumbling Underground, it was a simple brick structure for the servants of the St Paul's Knightsbridge congregation. Decoration began within 20 years and soon St Mary's also had titled people in its congregation.

The original entrance was in Graham Terrace rather than Bourne Street which only received its name in 1938. Today's main doorway in Bourne Street was created in the 1920s by the demolition of a house and erection of a polygonal porch designed by H. S. Goodhart-Rendel who was also responsible for converting the adjoining Pineapple pub into the presbytery.

The first vicar to live there was Humphrey Whitby who, over 32 years, consolidated the catholic tradition and high standard of liturgy with an adherence to the Prayer Book, though few recognized it, presented with Roman ceremonial. The preacher at Fr Whitby's funeral in 1948 was Robert Mortimer, the last diocesan bishop to wear liturgical gloves.

The focus of the church is Goodhart-Rendel's domed tabernacle behind the high altar. Above is a reredos by composer Charles Parry's nephew, S. Gambier Parry, but enhanced by both Martin Travers and Goodhart-Rendel. The apse panelling was added in 1974 by Roderick Gradidge with Gavin Stamp providing the lettering. Gradidge was a long-standing worshipper here and his ashes are buried in the columbarium which he designed shortly before his death. In its centre is a reliquary for a fragment of the True Cross.

In 1979 Princess Margaret was present at Solemn Benediction. In 1995 Cardinal Godfried Danneels of Brussels came to a Solemn Evensong marking the 70th anniversary of the Malines Conversations, an early attempt at Christian unity pioneered by Lord Halifax who was churchwarden from 1909 until his death in 1934. His memorial just inside the door states that he 'spent his life in defence of the Catholic truth and in labour for the reunion of Christendom'.

Daily Mass continues to be often enhanced by the use of vestments older than the church. One set belonged to a cardinal. Surprisingly, there was the occasional

St Mary's, Bourne Street

use of a facing altar here as early as the 1950s. The music is considered to be of an even higher standard than in the last century.

Recently attendance has risen leading to the reintroduction of a children's Mass. Although many people travel miles to worship here, at least 50 regulars can be described as local. Some people come to 'Bourne Street' just for the great feast days such as Corpus Christi when a freshly laid herb carpet releases an aroma as the blessed sacrament is carried in procession around a church misty with incense.

Open Tuesday, Wednesday and Thursday 9.30am to 3.30pm
Bourne Street SW1W 8JJ
www.stmarythevirgin.org.uk

66
St Mary's, Holly Place
Roman Catholic

Holly Place is a recessed terrace with a tiny church in the centre. Inside there is just an aisle with a gallery at the back.

The church, one of the most attractive and mysterious in London, was built in 1816 having been founded by a French priest, Abbé Jean-Jacques Morel, for refugees from the 1789 Revolution. St Mary's is London's oldest post-Reformation Roman Catholic church and was deliberately blended with the houses in order not to draw any attention to itself. But the choice of 'Mary' reflects the original dedication of the parish church, St John's, at the bottom of Holly Hill.

An early visitor to the new St Mary's was the Duchesse d'Angoulême, daughter of Louis XVI and Marie Antoinette, who was just one of many refugees who remained in England.

The chapel's Tuscan bellcote and niche for Our Lady was added in 1850 when anti-Catholic laws had been repealed and the climate of tolerance became more evident. Parishioner William Wardell oversaw the new frontage shortly before emigrating to Australia where he was responsible for new cathedrals in Melbourne and Sydney.

His last task in England was the tomb memorial for Fr Morel who died in 1852. His actual tomb is at the west door. The side chapels, one of which now holds the Morel memorial, were added in 1907 along with the east end mosaic walls. The high altar *baldacchino* erected in 1935 is by Adrian Gilbert Scott, and was the result of his daughter Margaret Powell being a member of the congregation. The stations of the cross, completed in 1954, are by woodcarver Gino Masero.

In 1867 Charles Dickens and Edward Landseer came to the funeral of artist Clarkson Stanfield whose son Francis wrote the hymn 'Sweet sacrament divine'. Baron Friedrich von Hügel, the philosopher and theologian, worshipped here between 1876 and 1903. General de Gaulle always sat in the front row at the 11am Sunday Mass during his World War Two exile when he lived in nearby Frognal.

Graham Greene was married here in 1927. Ian Richardson and Alec McCowen were ushers in 1971 when Judi Dench and Michael Williams, who lived on this hill, arrived on foot for their wedding.

The presbytery, where Abbé Morel lived, is next door at number 4. Neighbours

St Mary's, Holly Place

in the row have included Frank Podmore, the founder member of the Fabian Society who chose its name, at number 6, and composer Sir William Walton at number 10.

The church, which lies at the top of St John's churchyard extension, is only open for Saturday evening Mass and on Sunday from 11am to 1pm when a Mass is celebrated at 11.30am

Holly Place NW3 6QU
www.rcdow.org.uk/hampstead

67

St Mary-le-Bow, Cheapside

Anglican

The 224-foot tower rises on the south side of Cheapside where the church has its grand entrance directly on to the pavement. A flower seller on the steps and cafe tables along the southern outside wall add to the foreign feel on hot summer days.

This is a restored Wren church with a crypt dating from 1087. Bow is a reference to the arches in the crypt where the Court of Arches, an ecclesiastical court, sits occasionally. The church came directly under Canterbury until 1850.

Hollar called it 'Boo Church' in his panorama. Wren would recognize the crypt and tower today, but the main church, damaged in 1941 by World War Two bombing, has been rebuilt largely to his plan by Laurence King. There is a feeling of simplicity and light enhanced by a large rood cross suspended from the ceiling and pale windows. Both are by John Hayward whose controversial west window for Sherborne Abbey was an issue before the court downstairs. One window shows the Virgin holding a model of the church.

The Great Bell of Bow in the tower rings out at midday on Ascension Day to remind the City that the day is special. Claims that the bells helped to call Dick Whittington back from the bottom of Highgate Hill may not be far-fetched. In the fourteenth century there was little noise pollution and bells could be heard miles away. A recording, broadcast by the BBC during the war as a morale booster, was heard in Norway – which explains why there is a Norwegian Chapel.

There is a bust of early Australian settler Admiral Arthur Phillip who was baptized here, and Australians come for an Australia Day service. There is also a link with New York's Trinity Wall Street which when founded in 1697 was 'ordered as it is in the Church of St Mary-le-Bow'. A cherub head found in the blitzed rubble at St Mary-le-Bow is now over Trinity's Cherub Gate.

Cardinal Pole came here in 1557 to receive the pallium and today new diocesan bishops in the Canterbury province come to have their election confirmed and to take the Oath of Allegiance in the presence of the Archbishop of Canterbury.

The twin pulpits were designed for lunchtime dialogues began in 1964 by rector Joseph McCulloch and revived by Victor Stock, whose outstanding ministry re-opened the church to visitors. Actress Diana Rigg and former Cabinet Secretary Lord Wilson are among those who have debated here, and sometimes provided

St Mary-le-Bow, Cheapside

surprise insights. Joan Bakewell, another participant, was married here.

The church is also known for its music and dignified minimalist liturgy. There are no Sunday services for this is a mission to commuters with important weekday holy days marked by a lunchtime High Mass.

But the church is also visited by City workers wanting lunch in the award-winning cafe below in the crypt.

Open Monday to Thursday 7.30am to 6pm; Friday 7.30am to 4pm
Cheapside EC2V 6AU
www.stmarylebow.co.uk

68
St Mary-le-Strand

Anglican

There is traffic on both sides but the island site manages to sustain two magnolias. The church is narrow but John Betjeman called it a 'baroque paradise'.

The first church, dedicated to The Nativity of Our Lady & the Innocents of The Strand, stood to the south on land now occupied by Somerset House. Indeed, when the church was forcibly demolished in 1548 its stone was used for the Duke of Somerset's new house.

The congregation used the Queen's Chapel of the Savoy for over 150 years until in 1711 Queen Anne's Act for building new churches allowed for a replacement. The foundation stone was laid in 1715 just after George I had come to the throne and his coat of arms was above the chancel arch for the opening in 1724.

This was the first church by architect James Gibbs, a Roman Catholic who had trained in Rome under the papal architect Carlo Fontana. The west end entrance resembles Rome's Santa Maria della Pace while inside the ceiling is inspired by those at S Apostoli and SS Luca e Martina. But the east end is a smaller version of St Paul's Cathedral and at first had plain glass.

The idea of a spire came later so it is slender to avoid extra weight. The high side windows indicate the attempt to exclude the sound of carriage wheels on cobbles.

The chancel has paintings by the American artist Mather Brown who had been a pupil of Benjamin West. The present altar was made in 1994 and follows the proportions of the original communion table.

In 1750 Bonnie Prince Charlie came here from exile to be received into the Church of England. Weddings include Charles Dickens' parents in 1809.

The catholic tradition was established by Dr Alfred Bowen Evans who was rector from 1861 to 1878. He worked with architect R. J. Withers to turn box pews into the present seating arrangement. A more recent incumbent was Derek White who was also the Bishop of London's chaplain to the homeless.

In 1982 a block of stone fell from the tower and the *Evening Standard* front page warned that the spire might have to be removed. Two years later, in Christian Heritage Year, London Transport featured the church on a poster by Glynn Boyd Harte.

The parish, which incorporates St Clement Danes and has around 600 residents,

St Mary-le-Strand

embraces the Royal Courts of Justice, the London School of Economics and Bush House. On Palm Sunday the outdoor procession sets out from India House.

There is a Sung Eucharist on Sunday morning and lunchtime celebrations on weekdays. Since 1982 this has been the Wrens' Church, with former members of the Women's Royal Naval Service holding a carol service here. An annual event since the 1920s is the Eucharist on the anniversary of Charles I's execution, when a painting of the King and Queen Henrietta Maria is displayed.

Open Monday to Saturday 11am to 4pm
Strand WC2R 1ES
www.stmarylestrand.org

69

St Mary's, Monken Hadley

Anglican

The church tower is the focal point of a rural hamlet with Georgian houses on Enfield Chase. This is so far from central London that as late as 1972 the Byng family of nearby Wrotham Park maintained a second home in St James's Square. With a bench mark in the church wall being on a line with the cross on the top of St Paul's Cathedral, the parish affords views south across London.

Behind the tower is a small country church filled with memorials and patrolled by a cat. Electricity was not installed until 1931 and now light is provided by a chandelier given by former Home Secretary Robert Carr.

Monken refers to the monks of Walden Abbey who were given a hermitage here in 1136 by the first Earl of Essex Geoffrey de Mandeville. The first church was probably built around 1244.

It was from here that clergy ministered to the injured of the Battle of Barnet on Easter Day 1471 when Warwick the Kingmaker was among the 1,000 dead. The battle, fought in the village, ended the Wars of the Roses and led within 14 years to Henry VII becoming King. His household treasurer Sir Thomas Lovell rebuilt the church in 1494. The date appears in arabic numerals above the door below the tower.

This Tudor tower is topped by a unique copper beacon said to have been lit as part of a chain of lights to warn of the Spanish Armada. Igniting, which involves a long preparation with oily rags, is reserved for special occasions such as the Queen's Jubilee.

The dedication in 1504 was recorded as St Mary & St James, the latter being the patron of Saffron Walden, and this is recognized with a window depicting both together. A St Catherine Chapel survives in a transept.

The 'Mary window' behind the high altar, installed in 1952, is by Francis Stephens and depicts the Virgin from her birth in St Anne's bed to her Assumption.

The present look of the interior owes much to G. E. Street's restoration that was completed in 1850. The church then was under Tractarian influence and attracting around 200 people on a Sunday morning. Anthony Trollope, who was living here, described the church in his novel *The Bertrams* where the main characters attend the morning service.

The brasses include one from the old church. Behind the main door are memorial

St Mary's, Monken Hadley

busts by Nicholas Stone of Sir Roger Wilbraham, who built nearby almshouses in 1616, and his wife.

The churchyard is planted with snowdrops, celandines and lavender and has the graves of Trollope's sister Emily, and William Thackeray's grandparents. The attractive Gate House to Enfield Chase is the official residence of the parish clerk and verger.

Morning prayer is said daily and Sunday's main worship is usually a Sung Eucharist. Evensong survives and the choir has sung this Anglican service at Roman Catholic St Joseph's Highgate and even Bologna Cathedral in Italy.

Open on the second Sunday in the month 2.30pm to 4pm
Hadley Common EN5 5QD
www.stmarymh.co.uk

70

St Mary, Moorfields

Roman Catholic

The church is easily missed in Eldon Street by commuters walking to Liverpool Street Station. There is a doorway flanked by shops, but only if you look up do you see some interesting decoration which hints at the church beyond.

This is on a lower level than the street and lit only by high small windows. At the far end is a blue marble backdrop with six 18-foot-high marble columns framing an altar that resembles a bath. It is as if this is a church built in penal times and therefore deliberately camouflaged. But this is the opposite of the situation for the church was built only in 1903 as a substitute for a triumphalist first church.

This extraordinary interior is the result of the salvaging of parts of that original church which stood nearby on the corner of Bloomfield Street from 1817 to 1899. It would have been the first landmark seen by passengers emerging from Broad Street Station. The spot is now marked by a plaque that is often hidden by copies of the *Evening Standard* stacked up in an alcove on the street corner. To appreciate the impressive frontage one must visit St John the Baptist in Brighton where the front is modelled on the first St Mary Moorfields.

The first architect was John Newman who incorporated elements of Saint Sulpice in Paris. The church was grand enough to become the temporary cathedral for the first Archbishop of Westminster, Cardinal Wiseman. The great feature of the church was its panorama of the crucifixion by scene painter Agostino Aglio, which covered the curved marble wall behind the altar. According to Augustus Pugin, it was 'like a theatre'.

Demolition of the old church in 1900 was partly a result of structural damage caused by the Underground railway and a drop in population. The new church was designed by George Sherrin who incorporated in small scale the main elements of the old sanctuary, including the distinctive altar intended as a sarcophagus for Cardinal Wisemen. A copy of the panorama was added but unfortunately this giant painting with larger than life figures was removed for renovation in 1964 and never seen again. The search is ongoing, and the marble sanctuary remains as bare as a bathroom.

Although in 1924 the parish priest Mgr Edmond Nolan was chaplain to the Lord Mayor, it was another 70 years before this church was able once more to call itself a City church thanks to a favourable change in the Corporation of London

St Mary, Moorfields

boundary. It is a City church with a Sunday congregation and is popular for Saturday weddings as it can look full with just 50 guests. But on the rare weekday holy day of obligation there is standing room only as more than 200 City workers pack the church for each Mass.

Open daily 6.45am to 6.45pm
Eldon Street EC2M 7LS
www.stmarymoorfields.net

71

St Mary's, Primrose Hill

Anglican

This red brick church stands at the bottom of Primrose Hill in an area of imposing Victorian family houses, substantial council flats and a tower block.

St Mary's has its origins in a Hampstead mission to the poor in the form of an iron church. The present building, standing on land given by Eton College, opened in 1872. The architect was M. P. Manning, a member of the temporary church congregation who worked closely with the first vicar, Charles Fuller. Twenty years later, under the second vicar, Albert Spencer, the building was finished with the addition of the Chapel of the Holy Spirit, south aisle, vestries and ambulatory.

Once completion approached, G. F. Bodley was commissioned to provide the

The cat window in St Mary's

pulpit, choir stalls and reredos. A north aisle window depicts St Sidwell, patron of Fr Spencer's previous parish in Exeter. Anthony Hardcastle, vicar from 1934 to 1951, is remembered by his cat William in an apse window.

The white interior of the church was the idea in 1903 of Percy Dearmer, the most famous vicar. The Catholic faith had been taught despite episcopal disapproval and Fr Dearmer, who inherited a 400-strong congregation, made the church an example of good practice. 'You must give people what is good and they will come to like it,' claimed this influential twentieth-century priest.

Dearmer was the driving force behind the at first unpopular *English Hymnal* which was an alternative to *Hymns Ancient & Modern*. Many now familiar hymns were tried out in this church. 'In the bleak midwinter' was first heard in December 1905 at a Friday night congregational

hymn practice. In 1908 Dearmer recruited the composer Martin Shaw as
organist and together they co-operated
on the equally influential *Oxford Book
of Carols*.

The vicar introduced Sarum Plainsong, as well as writing his own hymn,
'Jesus, good above all other'. As recently
as the 1960s the choir was still male
with a mainly plainsong repertoire. The
association with the *English Hymnal*
continued with Howard Hollis, vicar
from 1965 to 1976, and director of the
English Hymnal Company, and his tune
'Edenhall', named after a Hampstead
hospice, is included in *English Praise*.
George Timms, a former vicar, became
editor of the *New English Hymnal*
published in 1986.

Some Dearmer vestments are still in
use but the liturgy has been allowed to
develop. In 1981 the altar was moved
forward in accordance with western
development and there are now boy
and girl servers.

In 2007 the building was extended
east with the addition of the St Mary's
Centre where the parish runs a social
inclusion programme for young people,

St Mary's, Primrose Hill

reflecting the original mission. Today's congregation is largely drawn from the
local area with 22 different languages spoken.

On Palm Sunday the congregation gathers on top of Primrose Hill for the
procession into the church. Sunday evening service is Prayer Book choral evensong
or Taizé music and prayers.

Open Monday to Friday 9am to 2pm
Elsworthy Road NW3 3DJ
www.smvph.org.uk

72

St Mary's, Putney

Anglican

St Mary's stands by the Thames Path and at the south end of Putney Bridge, which can be seen from inside the church through the window behind the altar which unusually is on the north side. Inland there is a new piazza used for markets and processions.

An extraordinary feature inside the church is the fan-vaulted Bishop West Chapel which was probably built during Henry VIII's reign by masons who had worked on St George's Chapel at Windsor. West had been dean there and this was his home church. His father was a Putney fishmonger. The son had become Bishop of Ely but his important and dangerous role was as chaplain to Katharine of Aragon whom he supported while her husband disowned her. As can be seen from his arms, both the Bishop and Queen shared the pomegranate as a badge.

Also unique is the Putney Debates exhibition which records the Cromwellian debates held in the church in 1647. The participants allegedly sat round the altar with their hats on. More significant is that the American constitution owes much to the ideas raised during the debates.

The tower is fifteenth century while the main building is mainly a very early Victorian enlargement by E. Lapidge. Indeed the entire Bishop West Chapel was moved from the south to north side in 1837. The latest arrangement was made possible by a fire in 1973 which allowed the bold re-ordering by Ronald Sims completed in 1982.

The space where the altar stood was for a time filled with *The Last Supper* by Damien Hirst. Here a glass screen can be pulled across to allow children to be seen and not heard during services.

Samuel Pepys visited in 1667 when he heard a 'good sermon'. Edward Gibbon, author of *The Decline and Fall of the Roman Empire*, was christened here in 1737. Charles Dickens knew the church and he made it the setting for David Copperfield's wedding.

Seats on three sides of the new altar are packed with families for the Eucharist on Sundays which lasts under an hour. This is a very successful modern church in the catholic tradition. On Palm Sunday there is an outdoor procession with a donkey through the parish to the church. Many Putney organizations meet at the

St Mary's, Putney

church. Visiting preachers have included the controversial American Bishop Gene Robinson.

Indeed many see St Mary's as an inspiring model parish church with good liturgy, noted preaching and extensive pastoral care. Much of this reputation is due to broadcaster and academic Giles Fraser who was vicar for almost a decade until 2009.

The church entrance is by way of a good-value cafe in a glass building where the latest magazines and daily papers are available to be enjoyed with an all-day breakfast. 'The truth is that, without the fire, we would not be half the church we are today,' admitted Canon Fraser.

Open daily
Putney Bridge SW15 1SL
www.allsaintsputney.co.uk

73
St Mary's, Rotherhithe
Anglican

The Georgian church is wedged between riverside warehouses and an early eighteenth-century charity school house. The interior has been adapted to liturgical changes introduced in the nineteenth century.

There was Roman occupation here and a church from at least 1282 was served by monks from Bermondsey Abbey.

The present church, on foundations that include Tudor bricks, was mainly built between 1714 and 1716. The architect was John James who had worked with Nicholas Hawksmoor and was soon to design St George's in Hanover Square which was completed long before the tower of St Mary's was finally built in 1747.

The organ was built and installed by John Byfield in 1764 and the clock on the front of the organ gallery was made by a local clockmaker and installed in the following year.

Built to seat 1,000 people, there were galleries, box pews, and a large three-tiered pulpit until 1876 when William Butterfield was asked to re-order the inside.

The east window is a sixteenth-century stained glass representation of the Assumption of Our Lady brought from Germany earlier in the nineteenth century.

The nearby Finnish, Norwegian and Swedish churches were built to serve visiting sailors and the parish church has had a congregation also mainly involved in shipping and the river. Indeed the pillars of the church are said to be ships' masts.

A brass plate commemorates Peter Hills who was Master of Trinity House in 1593. The memorial to Captain Charles Wood was made in 1625 by 'the King's Carver in His Majesty's Yards at Deptford and Woolwich'. A tablet at the east end recalls Captain Christopher Jones of *The Mayflower* who took the

Interior of St Mary's

St Mary's, Rotherhithe

Pilgrim Fathers to America in 1620 and is buried in the churchyard. His children were baptized in the church.

The two bishops' chairs are made from timber salvaged from the ship *Temeraire*. The ship was broken up here in 1838 and made famous by Turner's painting *The Fighting Temeraire towed to her last berth*, which is now in the National Gallery.

Wood from the *Temeraire* was also used for the communion table in the side chapel. But its wooden reredos depicting the Epiphany was made in Oberammergau and comes from the nearby Clare College mission church which closed in 1966.

In the churchyard there is a 1995 statue of Captain Jones. Rotherhithe and its church is naturally special to Americans and this modern work by Jamie Sargeant was presented by The Sons and Daughters of the Pilgrims. Also here is Prince Lee Boo of Palau, a Pacific island, who travelled to England with Rotherhithe sailors who were returning home in 1784.

The parish has many flats in warehouse conversions and new houses. It also embraces Surrey Quays Shopping Centre at Canada Water and Surrey Docks Farm. The catholic tradition established in the 1870s is maintained, with a focus on the Sunday parish Mass.

Open daily
Church Street, Rotherhithe SE16 4JE
www.stmaryrotherhithe.org

74

St Marylebone Parish Church

Anglican

Marylebone's parish church is known for its landmark cupola which was once visible during BBC London weather forecasts. But the building with its six-column portico is best seen from just inside Regent's Park and framed by its York Gate.

Marylebone is derived from Mary-le-burne, a reference to the Tyburn river which flowed to the west of the church. The interior of an earlier building was portrayed by Hogarth in *The Rake's Progress*.

The present church on a new site is by Thomas Hardwicke and was opened in 1817, but was much improved in 1884 when most of the double gallery was removed. These changes were overseen by churchwarden and architect Thomas Harris. Outside can be found the second foundation stone laid by 'Mrs Gladstone', wife of William Gladstone.

Fragments of coloured glass, blown out during World War Two, now decorate the edge of plain windows, allowing plenty of light into the church. The two crystal chandeliers in the nave came from the Marylebone Council Chamber. An oil painting of the Holy Family by local resident Benjamin West once hung behind the altar. Now this is in the intimate Holy Family Chapel where the crib is placed at Christmas.

The Browning Room, where babies can cry freely during services, commemorates the secret wedding of poet Robert Browning and Elizabeth Barrett in 1746. Other weddings in the earlier buildings include Francis Bacon in 1606, Sheridan in 1773, and Byron in 1788. Horatia, daughter of Lord Nelson and Lady Hamilton, was baptized in 1803. Charles Dickens, who lived next door to the present building, used the christening of his son Alfred in 1846 when describing a scene in his novel *Dombey and Son*. The funeral of actress and parishioner Wendy Richard was held here in 2009.

Among the rectors is Charles Wesley's acquaintance John Harley whose family gave its name to Harley Street. In the twentieth century Christopher Hamel Cooke conceived the idea of a healing ministry and, after 850 bodies had been removed, the crypt was opened in 1987 as the Healing and Counselling Centre with an NHS surgery and a cafe. Appropriately, memorial services upstairs have included the Queen's doctor George Pinker.

The adjoining St Marylebone Church of England School is one of the best in

St Marylebone Parish Church

London. The University of Westminster, the Methodist Church HQ and most of Regent's Park are in the parish.

There is a professional choir at the Sunday morning Eucharist which has a large congregation including many children. John Stainer's oratorio *The Crucifixion* was written for the choir in 1886 and is performed every Good Friday. The Austrian Rieger organ is played daily by students from the nearby Royal Academy of Music. There are regular healing services and a Nigerian congregation meets monthly in the afternoon.

Behind the school, in Marylebone High Street, is the site of the old church with the tombs of hymn-writer Charles Wesley, architect James Gibbs and painter George Stubbs.

Open Monday to Friday 10am to 4pm
Marylebone Road NW1 5LT
www.stmarylebone.org

75
St Matthew's, Westminster
Anglican

St Matthew's appears squeezed by flanking buildings and the inside is a warren of spaces alongside a courtyard.

The church was built between 1849 and 1851, with Westminster Abbey contributing £1,000. The architect was George Gilbert Scott who was assisted by his brother-in-law, G. F. Bodley. The adjoining clergy house was designed by Sir George's son, John Oldrid Scott.

The church seen today opened in 1984 and is the result of a bold restoration by Donald Buttress after an arson attack in 1977. The upstairs Lady Chapel, which had been added in 1892 by Comper, survives – along with its riddle-post English altar which was the first such revival since the Reformation.

But downstairs the church has been turned round and reduced in size. Here is a reredos depicting numerous saints around the nativity by Walter Tower and stations of the cross by Eric Gill's pupil, Joseph Cribb. A surprise is the 1698 pulpit which once stood in the now closed St Mary Lambeth. The high altar contains a relic of St Matthew brought from Salerno Cathedral in 1984.

There are modern statues of Our Lady by Mother Concordia and artist-in-residence Guy Reid. The latter's work is sometimes deemed controversial for its lack of clothing. The Requiem Chapel has a stone altar by Bodley.

At the entrance to the church is a memorial to Bishop Frank Weston who was a curate here from 1896 to 1898. Then it was already a leading Anglo-Catholic church with a Sunday congregation of more than 500, including over 200 children. Here in 1900 Spencer Jones preached a sermon which led to the instigation in 1908 of the annual Week of Prayer for Christian Unity.

This is the parish church of government departments, the Labour and Liberal Parties, Church House and New Scotland Yard. An important part of life is St Matthew's School, serving the families living on the Peabody estate and in other residential enclaves.

Regular worshippers have included Secret Intelligence Service head, Sir Maurice Oldfield, reputed model for John Le Carré's George Smiley, who sometimes played the organ. More recently former government minister Jonathan Aitken has been among the many, being a writer-in-residence here.

Cardinal Basil Hume, who gave the congregation temporary accommodation

St Matthew's, Westminster

in Westminster Cathedral after the fire, preached in the restored church. Rowan Williams worshipped here during Christmas 2002 prior to being enthroned as Archbishop of Canterbury.

There are monthly lunchtime recitals. Annual services include the Society of St Willibrord's Festival Eucharist attended by Anglicans and Old Catholics from Europe. The organization Affirming Catholicism, which had an office here, has held services and conferences.

There is a Sunday Solemn Eucharist, daily Mass and a weekly school Mass. The church, which is the centre of a community extending far beyond Westminster, has as its slogan 'working for the Kingdom of God'.

Open daily
Great Peter Street SW1P 2BU
www.stmw.org

76
St Michael's, Bedford Park
Anglican

The Queen Anne-style building with a roof balustrade is a landmark outside Turnham Green Underground station and the centrepiece of Bedford Park. A large inviting porch leads into a green and red Arts and Crafts nave where the view is a wooden rood at the high sanctuary steps.

Bedford Park is the original garden suburb and St Michael's was among the first buildings to be designed by its principal architect, Norman Shaw. Both the church and the matching Tabard Inn and shop opposite were opened in 1880 as essential infrastructure.

For the first decade one of the churchwardens was *Building News* editor Maurice B. Adams who helped Shaw to complete the church. Indeed Adams designed the north aisle in sympathy and added such furniture as the pulpit and font. He even included a bishop's throne. In 1909 his All Souls Chapel, which has a Martin Travers' stained glass window depicting St Michael slaying the dragon over London, provided balance to the building.

The other churchwarden was artist F. Hamilton Jackson who taught at the village's Adams-designed art school and drew a view of the vicarage, pub and church for an advertisement promoting Bedford Park's new houses. The vicarage architect was Shaw's pupil E. J. May who produced a large family house with generous fireplaces and windows in keeping with the other residences being erected at the time.

St Michael's commitment to the catholic revival was confirmed when the foundation stone was laid by Lord Nelson and by the presence at the opening of the temporary church of such Anglo-Catholic pioneers as T. Pelham Dale from St Vedast and Fr Arthur Tooth. Today St Michael's is a beacon of modern catholicism with good liturgy and music.

The church and its exterior can be seen in the 1990 film *Nuns on the Run* starring Robbie Coltrane. On Sunday the painted Norman Shaw pews, complete with armrests, are filled by many who live nearby.

There are daily services and the high points of the liturgical year are observed with care, especially Holy Week which starts with an outdoor palm procession and ends with a large fire being lit on the grass outside for a 5am Easter Vigil.

Another major occasion in the year is St Michael's Day on 29 September when

St Michael's, Bedford Park

the church welcomes regular annual visitors and a noted preacher. A highlight of the patronal festival is the Children's Church performing its popular 'Skirmish' when the dragon is driven out of the church by the children acting the part of St Michael or his angels.

In the summer the Bedford Park Festival, organized by the church for over 40 years, has a two-week programme of outdoor events, concerts, talks and art exhibitions culminating in a Festive Choral Mass complete with orchestra. Celebrity openers have included Sir Peter Blake, John Humphrys and Sophie Ellis-Bextor.

A recent project has been a careful remodelling of the parish hall, with thousands of pounds still raised for charity outside the parish.

Open daily
Bath Road w4 1TT
www.smaaa.org.uk

77
St Michael's, Camden Town
Anglican

The brick and stone church in the main shopping street is now known as 'the church next to Sainsbury's'. The largely stone interior, described by *The Times* as 'glorious neo-gothic', is lofty and slightly distressed.

St Michael's is the successor to the City church of St Michael Queenhithe which had been demolished in 1877. The sale of its materials funded most of the nave of the new church which was the first in London to be designed by Bodley and Garner. The nave was completed in 1882 and the chancel was added a decade later, allowing the building to be eventually consecrated in 1894. A planned tower was never built.

It is a tight site with the supermarket's trolley park being the best place to view the flying buttresses, although they give little clue to the tall clerestory best appreciated from inside. A low vaulted north-east chapel is now reserved for prayer. The building has very good acoustics.

But the parish is now much larger than in Victorian times having not only taken over next-door All Saints, where the building is now a Greek Orthodox Cathedral, and St Thomas Agar Town, which was demolished due to war damage, but also by becoming the mother church of a new Old St Pancras parish which includes the original St Pancras Church and St Paul's, Camden Square.

For many years St Michael's was locked and ignored by the majority of the Camden Town residents. In the early 1990s a worker in the Labour Party office opposite said that he had never seen the church open. It was the appointment of Nicholas Wheeler as priest-in-charge in 1996 which brought dramatic change. His induction involved the longest outdoor church procession on record.

The west front was restored in 2005 and the roof replaced in 2007 after curate Malcolm Hunter, a former builder, spent ten sponsored nights on the roof in order to quickly raise £100,000 which released match funding.

Fr Wheeler's tireless ten-year ministry even included once celebrating Mass in the nearby William Hill betting shop which is on the site of a temporary church where services were held before today's church was built.

In 2006 the Archbishop of Canterbury and the Archbishop of York chose to visit together to launch the Church of England's *Faithful Cities* report. The church also featured in *The Power and the Glory* television series.

St Michael's, Camden Town

Around 3,000 people visit the church each week and there is plenty of local information and teaching literature there. A Community Renewal Project provides a ministry to the homeless and refugees.

The Sunday morning Mass, where attendance has risen from six to well over a hundred, is crowded with people of all ages. There is also a Spanish Mass. But this building is not just for Sunday congregations, 'It belongs to Camden Town,' says the vicar.

Open Tuesday, Wednesday, Thursday and Friday afternoons
Camden Road NW1 9LQ
www.saintmichaelcamden.250x.com

78

St Michael's, Croydon

Anglican

Only in recent times has St Michael's found itself handily near an important tram junction and at the back door of the Whitgift shopping centre. The inside of the church is an oasis to be discovered in Croydon's teeming shopping and business area.

The huge London brick church is in the centre of a parish where one half is like a City parish, empty at night and weekends. The other half is beyond a railway line and has a rising residential population that includes many Muslims.

The church stands on land bought from the London, Brighton & South Coast Railway. The foundation stone was laid in 1880 by Lord Nelson, a great nephew of the Admiral. Just three years later the new Archbishop of Canterbury Edward Benson came to consecrate the 150-foot-long church designed by J. L. Pearson.

The architect was chosen for being in sympathy with the Anglo-Catholic founders of the new parish and he designed a building that he described as 'a place for real worship'. It has his recognizable soaring vaulting and distinctive ambulatory already found at the new Truro Cathedral and St Stephen's in Bournemouth. John Betjeman considered St Michael's to be 'one of Pearson's loveliest churches' and the severe critic Nikolaus Pevsner claimed the interior to be 'one of the most satisfying of its date anywhere'.

After Pearson's death G. F. Bodley designed the pulpit with the elaborate canopy topped with St Michael defeating the Devil.

The organ case above St George's Chapel is also Bodley's creation and the much admired 'Father Willis' organ comes from the temporary wooden church which stood on the site. Composer George Oldroyd was organist from 1921 to 1956 and came from St Alban's in Holborn, as did composer Michael Fleming in 1998 to rebuild the musical tradition. It is one of the few parish churches where plainsong psalmody is sung weekly and there are weekly organ recitals. The grand piano belonged to Ralph Vaughan Williams.

The dramatic 15-foot hanging rood above the chancel entrance was added in 1924. Five years afterwards the Lady Chapel was furnished by Comper and later its aumbry was designed by Francis Stephens.

Added in 2006 are the statues of St Michael and St James the Great which face each other across the nave. The latter is a reminder that the parish now includes

St Michael's, Croydon

the parish of the older but closed St James's Church.

In its first 125 years St Michael's has been visited by five Archbishops of Canterbury. There is a daily Mass. A Solemn Mass is celebrated not just on Sundays and the main holy days, but also on the Transfiguration in the holiday month of August and on St George's Day. People come from a distance but it is still a serious parish church with a family Mass and around 4,500 homes receiving a hand-delivered Christmas card. The new parish centre includes the Angel Cafe open on weekdays for coffee and lunches.

Open Monday to Friday 9.30am to 3pm
Poplar Walk CRO 1UA
www.stmichaelscroydon.org

79
St Michael Paternoster Royal, College Street

Anglican

The flat-fronted church stands at the bottom of College Hill where the houses have double gates and courtyards, as if in Italy. But the large church exterior is deceptive for the inside is surprisingly small.

It was known as St Michael Paternoster as early as 1219 when there were rosary makers working nearby. 'Royal' was added by 1361 to acknowledge the riverside parish's trading link with La Réole in France's Entre Deux Mers wine region.

Within 30 years Dick Whittington was living next door and in 1409 he rebuilt St Michael's, turning it into a collegiate church with the rector becoming the Master assisted by five clergy living as a community. This arrangement only lasted until 1548 but Whittington's almshouses on College Hill survive today as accommodation for 28 women at East Grinstead in Sussex.

Whittington's church was lost in the Great Fire and St Michael's was among the last to receive Wren's attention. The tower was not completed until 1713.

St Michael Paternoster Royal, College Street

This Wren replacement church was hit by a German flying bomb in 1944, leaving the walls and tower intact along with the altarpiece and the Grinling Gibbons pulpit.

It was only the Whittington connection that saved the church. The Corporation of London opposed a private Bill presented to Parliament by the Diocese of London for the sale of the building.

When St Michael Paternoster at last re-opened in 1968, having been remodelled by architect Elidir Davies, the side door had become the main door, opening on to the Whittington Garden. The west door on College Hill is now the entrance to Whittington Hall.

Whittington's tomb, unmarked for over 300

The Dick Whittington window

years, has been given the simple inscription 'Richard Whittington mercer 1358–1423'. A south window shows young Whittington and his cat in City streets paved with gold.

The glass is by John Hayward who also depicts St Michael overthrowing Satan in a dazzling window above the altar. This glass is flanked by his exceptionally bright windows showing the Virgin and Child and Adam and Eve.

A candelabra from the demolished All Hallows the Great hangs from the sky-blue ceiling.

Others buried here along with Whittington are Sir William Oldham, Speaker of the House of Commons, who died in 1459, and Peter Blundell whose 1601 will founded Blundell's School in Devon.

A banner featuring a flying angel reminds the visitor that this is now the central office of the Mission to Seafarers which co-ordinates the work of 300 chaplains worldwide. This explains the now small square church interior. The charity, in its hidden offices at the west end, has provided subsistence to sailors laid off as a result of the Iraq War and to sailor families who were victims of the 2004 Asian tsunami.

The Princess Royal, the Mission to Seafarers' patron, attends a service here at least once a year. There are no Sunday services.

Open Monday to Friday 9am to 5pm
College Street EC4R 2LR
www.missiontoseafarers.org

80
St Mildred's, Addiscombe
Anglican

St Mildred's is a tall brick church soaring above suburban houses. The inside is light. with an east window seen way beyond the high chancel. A modern addition manages not to intrude on the streetscape.

This is one of only seven churches in the British Isles dedicated to St Mildred who was Abbess of Minster in Kent. It can claim to be a successor to the now lost St Mildred's Bread Street in the City as the name was chosen by Thomas Bentham who had been curate there before coming to the mother church of St Mary Magdalene at Addiscombe.

St Mildred's is unusual in having a stone from Minster Abbey. The main foundation stone, laid in 1931 by the Archbishop of Canterbury Cosmo Gordon Lang, incorporates a fragment from Canterbury Cathedral. Other stones come from St Mary Magdalene out of which the parish was carved, and Croydon Parish Church.

The architect was G. F. Bodley's former partner Cecil Hare who died during the building work. Fortunately the vicar, Dr Charles Budden, already appointed to a temporary building, was an architecture graduate and able to take over supervision. At the time Croydon had the advantage of being a detached part of the Canterbury Diocese and so a year later the Archbishop returned for the consecration.

The sanctuary was added in 1934 followed in 1937 by the east end chapel which saw a third visit from the primate. Seventy years later, the west end was sympathetically extended with the addition of the St Mildred's Centre which includes a galleried hall, two kitchens and meeting rooms. In the middle there is a surprise round courtyard. The glass entrance has a welcome desk.

This development, the result of a sale of land which provides adjacent retirement homes, allows the church to continue to be a model for a residential parish, maintaining a pivotal role within the community. Archbishop Rowan Williams has described the centre as 'a very exciting new development'.

The church's once blue sanctuary was redecorated in its present extraordinary pink in 1957 when Archbishop Geoffrey Fisher visited. Princess Margaret came two years later.

Showcases contain the remnants of a remarkable museum once housed in a building that has given way to the new flats. The collection included Egyptian

St Mildred's, Addiscombe

antiquities now displayed in the British Museum, thousands of seashells, 100 Bibles and stuffed animals.

The choir, which has a long association with the Royal School of Church Music, regularly sings as holiday cover at Chichester, Lichfield and Winchester Cathedrals. Celebrity concerts in church in the past have featured a Rosalind Runcie piano recital, and former Prime Minister Ted Heath conducting.

Morning prayer is said daily. There is a Sunday school, a young people's group, and even a football academy.

The St Mildred's Centre is a venue for lunch clubs, pre- and after-school clubs, a long-standing literary society and a Peace, Justice & Environment Group.

Open daily
Bingham Road CRO 7EB
www.stmildredschurch.org.uk

81
Notre Dame de France, Leicester Square
Roman Catholic

Notre Dame de France, almost always known as the 'French Church', is wedged between Soho and Leicester Square and surrounded by clubs and restaurants.

The original church opened in 1868 in a converted panorama which accounts for the round shape. Empress Eugénie made a donation for this church intended for fellow exiles from France. The architect was Louis Auguste Boileau who at the time was working on Paris' Bon Marché department store.

Bombing in 1940 led to the new dramatic building by Hector O. Corfiato. In 1953 the first stone, from Chartres Cathedral, was laid by Maurice Schumann who had been the 'Voice of France' broadcasting from London. The Archbishop of Paris presided at the opening two years later.

The figure of the Virgin above the entrance is the work of George Saupique whose sculptures decorate the Palais du Trocadéro in Paris.

Inside the round church it is like a theatre with a gallery looking like a circle of boxes. Entrance pillars, ambos and a Saint Joseph statue were made by Beaux-Arts students.

But this is not a church of worship in the round, for the sanctuary, cleaned and restored in 2003, is at the east end below a giant tapestry by Dom Robert de Chaumac. Appropriately, for a church filled with art, the tapestry has along the bottom the words: 'I was by his side, like a master craftsman, ever at play in his presence'.

The Lady Chapel contains murals by Jean Cocteau who worked here for nine days in 1959. He started each day by lighting a candle and talked to the figures as he created their images. He told the Virgin depicted at the Annunciation: 'O you, most beautiful of women, loveliest of God's creatures, you were the best loved. So I want you to be my best piece of work too . . . I am drawing you with light strokes . . . You are the yet unfinished work of Grace.'

Recently added to the chapel after being rediscovered in the church is a mosaic of Mary and the newly born Jesus by Boris Anrep. The Russian, who was born in 1883 in St Petersburg and died in Britain in 1959, was on the fringes of the Bloomsbury Group.

Notre Dame de France, Leicester Square

The font is Vosges stone. The latest artwork is a painting by Charlotte Cochrane of Joan of Arc presented in 2003.

In the gallery there is a statue of Our Lady of Victories which was reconstructed after the bombing. The head was parachuted into France in 1942 to be restored.

For a time this was a church for French au pairs and other temporary residents from France. Today, many are French-speaking permanent London residents but not necessarily from France. Refugees are drawn here by the compassionate ministry.

The church is once again, as at its foundation, in the care of Marist Fathers. Mass and Vespers are in English on weekdays and in French at weekends. There are regular exhibitions and concerts.

A bookshop sells Cocteau postcards and French literature.

Open daily
Leicester Place WC2H 7BX
www.notredamechurch.co.uk

82

St Pancras Old Church

Anglican

This little church with a Norman-style doorway lies hidden behind the station which took its name and made the saint famous. Each row of nave seats can only contain four people.

The dedication to an early Roman saint and an altar top dating from 600 suggests that there has been a church here from very early times. It has been claimed that St Augustine, who had lived near the Basilica of St Pancras in Rome, celebrated Mass here.

The church stands on high ground above the River Fleet now flowing unseen below the road outside. There was rebuilding in 1350 and, despite a major restoration in 1848 which added the 'Norman' porch, there is still evidence of Roman bricks and authentic Norman doorways. The sanctuary has a thirteenth-century piscina and sedilia. The font cover is early eighteenth century.

The church was restored in 1948 under the direction of Martin Travers and again 30 years later by Quinlan Terry who removed unnecessary clutter to regain the original simplicity.

At one time the church, which for centuries stood on open ground a mile outside London, served a huge area of scattered houses including Kentish Town and Highgate. The southern boundary stone can be seen outside Heal's in Tottenham Court Road.

The second wedding of clown Joseph Grimaldi took place here in 1801. There was a crowded funeral in 2000 for Royal Academician Norman Blamey who was a server and regularly exhibited portraits of the parish clergy in the RA Summer Exhibition.

J. S. Bach's and John Soane's graves are in the churchyard, and Mary Wollstone-craft was also buried here until her body was moved to Bournemouth. Her daughter Mary first met her husband Percy Shelley when he was visiting her mother's grave.

The churchyard is large because it includes the burial ground of St Giles-in-the-Fields. But it is not as big as it was as a result of being shaved at the edge twice by the railway in 1866 and 2002. On the first occasion the Bishop of London appointed the future novelist Thomas Hardy to oversee the exhumations. He recalled his task in his poem 'The Levelled Churchyard'. Today moved gravestones

St Pancras Old Church

are stacked round Hardy's Tree.

Refugees from the French Revolution were buried here and, in a dig to extend the station for Eurostar services, the body of the Archbishop of Narbonne, Arthur Dillon, complete with a set of porcelain dentures, was exhumed. In 2007, 200 years after his death in exile, his body was interred in his cathedral in France.

Following the arrival of Eurostar, St Pancras Old Church has twinned with the Gare du Nord parish church L'Eglise de St Vincent de Paul.

The large St Pancras New Church opposite Euston Station opened in 1822 as the successor to the Old Church which for a time fell into disuse. But it was soon needed again and parish church status was restored in 1863. It is now the oldest church of four combined Camden parishes and has a packed congregation every St Pancras Day, 12 May.

Open Monday to Friday noon to 3pm
Pancras Road NW1 1UL
oldstpancrasteam.wordpress.com

83
St Patrick's, Soho Square
Roman Catholic

The red brick Italian-style building with a campanile has a deep entrance, with an altar, leading to the main church. Basil Hume described St Patrick's as 'a delightful discovery to the chance visitor and a much loved haven of prayer and peace'. Alongside it is the Georgian presbytery.

The original church on this site, entered from Sutton Row, was the former music room in the garden of Carlisle House which had been used for extravagant masked balls hosted by Teresa Cornelys. This Venetian opera singer was notorious for having had a child by Casanova. Her guests at the masked balls included the Prince Regent.

The first church was opened in 1792, a year after the Catholic Relief Act was passed, by Fr Arthur O'Leary of Spanish Place (see page 96) for the many Irish living in the area. His 1802 memorial in the entrance says 'he wore himself out by his labours'.

The present church was completed in 1893 when the opportunity was taken to make the new west end in Soho Square into the main entrance. The architect was John Kelly who had been G. E. Street's assistant.

The font with angels holding shells comes from the first St Mary Moorfields (see page 140). Statues of St John Fisher and St Thomas More, replacing two larger versions which were stolen, were given by female impersonator Danny la Rue who was a server and made his acting debut at the age of nine in the Christmas pantomime.

The focus is a crucifixion painting by a Van Dyck pupil positioned above the main altar. There are numerous side chapels and a John Bosco altar is a reminder that the Irish were followed by a wave of Italian immigrants. The two boys playing with the statue of St Patrick's are based on two from the parish.

Tommy Steele was married here in 1960, with a crowd of 3,000 outside and Sid James inside among the invited guests. American radio broadcaster Archbishop Fulton Sheen often stayed at the parish house and attracted large numbers.

Now Mass is in English, Cantonese, Portuguese and Spanish. There is a large Brazilian congregation.

The Connaught Rangers memorial is a reminder of the original Irish connection. Eamon de Valera for a time visited every St Patrick's Day. There is a relic of St

St Patrick's, Soho Square

Oliver Plunkett which is brought out for the annual Tyburn Walk which passes through the square.

Major annual occasions are the blessing of shamrock on the eve of St Patrick's Day and Corpus Christi when an international Mass is followed by an outdoor procession to St Giles-in-the-Fields.

There is a trained choir for Sung Mass alternating between Latin and English settings. Congregational participation is encouraged. A gospel choir sings at Sunday evening Mass. The organ predates the first church, having been built for Carlisle House musical evenings.

St Patrick's has a community of priests, young people running an evangelization school, and a weekly open house where volunteers serve a meal to around 100 homeless people.

Open daily
Soho Square W1D 4NR
www.stpatricksoho.org

84
St Paul's, Covent Garden
Anglican

The grand portico in the Covent Garden piazza has no door so the porch has instead become a stage for street theatre. To enter the church one must walk through the delightful churchyard lit by gas lamps. The church interior is wide and quiet and often one of the cats, Inigo or Jones, is snoozing on a chair.

In 1629 the Earl of Bedford commissioned Inigo Jones to design a square with a church as the focal point at one end. Not wanting the building to cost too much, Lord Bedford suggested something 'not much better than a barn'. Jones responded by promising 'the handsomest barn in England'.

This was the first new church since the Reformation and building began before it was realized that the Tuscan portico could never be the main entrance as the altar had to go at the east end. The church had been built the wrong way round or on the wrong side of the square.

But this is still one of Inigo Jones' best buildings, much painted by Hogarth, and in 1973 it even appeared on a postage stamp. This is the Actors' Church and its architect was a costume and stage designer. Here many actors get married and many more are mourned. Leslie Phillips and Peter O'Toole even danced together in the church for the 2006 film *Venus*.

One of the first actors to worship here regularly was David Garrick. Baptisms include the artist J. M. W. Turner and W. S. Gilbert of Gilbert and Sullivan fame. World War Two cartoonist David Low was married here.

Buried here are Grinling Gibbons, whose carving of flowers is on the west end screen, actor Charles Macklin, and artist Thomas Rowlandson. Thomas Arne, who composed the tune for 'Rule Britannia', was both baptized and buried here. The ashes of the actress Ellen Terry are behind an Art Nouveau grill.

John Wesley described St Paul's as 'the largest and best constructed parish church' when he preached here. Now addresses are often given by stars at the numerous memorial services which have included the writer Beverley Nichols in 1983 and the actor John Inman in 2008. In 1983 Dick Emery's service was attended by his wife and girlfriend who sat on different sides of the church and never spoke. Alan Jay Lerner, creator of the *My Fair Lady* film which, faithful to Shaw, featured the portico, was patron of the church's 350th anniversary appeal. Naturally his memorial service was held here. In 1990 the entire *Upstairs Downstairs* cast was

St Paul's, Covent Garden

present for Gordon Jackson's funeral.

Among the plaques can be found the names of Charlie Chaplin, Gracie Fields and Ivor Novello. Michael Wilding's was unveiled by Dame Anna Neagle.

The Actors' Church Union, which co-ordinates theatre chaplaincies, is based here. Because Samuel Pepys saw the first Punch and Judy show outside the church on 9 May 1662 there is an annual Punch and Judy service with Mr Punch in the pulpit.

Open Monday to Friday
Bedford Street WC2E 9ED
www.actorschurch.org

85
St Paul's, Deptford

Anglican

'Everyone should visit St Paul's Church in Deptford before they die . . . it is London's forgotten Baroque jewel,' advised Richard Morrison in *The Times*. Thirty years ago the artist Geoffrey Fletcher was also enthusiastic: 'Its big Roman Doric columns are as dramatic as those of Bernini before St Peter's in Rome; these and the two lateral Baroque flights of steps, to say nothing of the interior, would put St Paul's on the tourist's map, if only it were in Italy.'

But it is in fact off Deptford High Street which still has two pie and mash shops. Tourists on their way from London Bridge to Greenwich by train briefly look down on this gem and think that they have arrived.

St Paul's was one of the 12 churches erected as a result of the 1711 Commission for building Fifty New Churches. Architect Thomas Archer began work in 1712. Although much of the structure was completed by 1720 craftsmen continued to be employed until 1730. Deptford already had an ancient church dedicated to the sailor, St Nicholas, but a huge second one was justified by a growing population and the busy port.

The condition and tradition of St Paul's has been carefully maintained thanks to a record Heritage Lottery Fund grant of almost £3 million. This church with giant columns is built with Portland stone and has a circular tower with an afterthought steeple. Like Archer's better-known but less grand church of St John's in Smith Square, it rests on a raised crypt which is mostly above ground. The entrance is derived from Santa Maria della Pace in Rome.

The inside is square with two side aisles each separated by two Corinthian columns. There are side galleries, with an organ gallery above the main entrance. The altar is below a curving Venetian window.

To one side is a memorial by Joseph Nollekens to Vice-Admiral James Sayer who first raised the British Flag on the island of Tobago.

Two rose windows commemorate David Diamond who was appointed rector in 1968 at the age of 33 and stayed until his death from exhaustion in 1992. He founded the Deptford Festival and was not only an influence in the life of the then poor community but an inspiration far beyond Deptford. He was visited by the Queen in her Silver Jubilee Year and also by the Queen Mother and Princess Margaret who supported his ministry.

St Paul's, Deptford

The church is a superb space for good liturgy and Fr Diamond exploited the setting. The tradition continues with the Easter fire on Holy Saturday night lit to be seen framed by the columns of the semicircular portico. At Corpus Christi there is a procession around the extensive walled churchyard scattered with table tombs.

St Paul's Sinfonia has been performing here since 2004 when restoration made the church once again so attractive.

Open Saturday morning
Deptford High Street SE8 3DS
www.paulsdeptford.org.uk

86
St Paul's, Knightsbridge
Anglican

The highly decorated and galleried Victorian brick building, hidden behind The Berkeley hotel, is not only convenient for fashionable weddings but claims to be the first in London to promote the ideals of the Oxford Movement to which it remains faithful. The church features in the books of Charlotte M. Yonge who was known as the 'novelist of the Oxford Movement'.

The building was consecrated in 1843. The original architect was the Grosvenor Estate surveyor Thomas Cundy but the chancel with its rood screen and striking reredos was added in 1892 by G. F. Bodley who was also responsible for the decoration of the St Luke's Chapel.

Prominent tiled panels around the walls of the nave, created in the 1870s by Daniel Bell, depict scenes from the life of Christ. The stations of the cross that intersperse them were painted in the early 1920s by Gerald Moira.

The first vicar was William Bennett who founded, amid much controversy, St Barnabas Pimlico at the poor end of the parish. At St Paul's he had a very well-attended choral Eucharist and introduced the congregation to plainsong.

St Paul's font

The standard of music remains so high that director of music Stephen Farr came from Guildford Cathedral to hold the same position at St Paul's. There are two choirs.

Guests at a recent marriage included the Countess of Wessex, Princess Eugenie, Princess Beatrice, Joan Collins and Geri Halliwell. In 1900 Winston Churchill witnessed his mother's controversial wedding when Lady Randolph Churchill married young Captain George Cornwallis-West. A year later his sister Shelagh came here to marry the Duke of Westminster.

Sixty-six years later Lady Spencer-Churchill attended the funeral of Commander C. R. Thompson who had been her husband's personal assistant at Downing Street from 1940 to 1945. Recent years have seen the funerals of journalist Ross Benson, thoroughbred racehorse owner Robert Sangster, Cabinet minister

St Paul's, Knightsbridge

John Profumo, and Annabel's nightclub owner Mark Birley when Prince and Princess Michael of Kent and Lady Thatcher attended.

The many memorial services include sculptress Barbara Hepworth, novelist Rose Macaulay, and the eccentric aristocrat Lord Michael Pratt.

Among the first members of the congregation were Prime Ministers the Duke of Wellington, who lived in the parish, and Lord John Russell. It remains a small parish with a few diplomatic missions but the church attracts large numbers. Princess Margaret attended in the early 1950s. More recently bookseller Tim Waterstone was a churchwarden.

Vicars who have lived at the very large 1871 clergy house next door include Edward Henderson who became Bishop of Bath and Wells. During the war the vicarage was lent to FANY (First Aid Nursing Yeomanry) which holds an annual memorial service here.

The processional cross is seen by millions every year at the televised Festival of Remembrance at the nearby Royal Albert Hall. There is daily Mass.

Open 9am to 6.30pm
Wilton Place SW1X 8SH
www.stpaulsknightsbridge.org

87

St Peter's, Eaton Square

Anglican

St Peter's is a large church with a six-columned Ionic portico and a clock tower. Inside is possibly the most modern and best equipped urban church in London.

Designed by Henry Hakewell, St Peter's was built between 1824 and 1827 during the early development of Eaton Square. After 160 years as a fashionable church, disaster struck in 1987 when an arsonist reduced the Georgian building to an open-air shell.

The blaze was seen by architects John and Nicki Braithwaite who were asked by rector Desmond Tillyer to take advantage of disaster and produce a dramatic re-ordering and restoration. The exterior has been preserved for the Belgravia streetscape but fitted inside the Greek revival building is not just a church with a gold mosaic apse but a school, youth club, offices, a hall and residences. The roof-top vicarage has an open-air fountain.

The scheme evolved from the skeleton of the building and has reversed Sir Arthur Blomfield's 1875 enlargement by returning the nave to its original Georgian size. The gallery has gone but side pews face inward and are raked.

Clear glass allows generous light in. Behind the east end is an ambulatory reminiscent of a cinema foyer but wide enough for processions on festival days. The Victorian sanctuary is now the vestry.

Victoria Station, the Spanish Embassy and Victoria Place are in the parish.

This may not be the official Royal Parish Church but Buckingham Palace is in this parish and the church can be seen across the garden from the Queen's upstairs windows. Her Majesty's farrier made a cross for the church with nails from the old roof. The Sunday congregation included many Palace residents in the days before the Queen spent her weekends at Windsor and staff stopped living-in seven days a week.

The Prince of Wales, the future Edward VII, attended a wedding here in 1882. In 1950 George VI and Queen Elizabeth with their daughter Princess Margaret came to the wedding of the Duke of Somerset's heir.

This was the wedding church. In the 1930s *Time* magazine told its readers that the marriage of Prince Ludwig of Hesse was at 'London's swank St Peter's Church, Eaton Square'. P. G. Wodehouse includes in his poem 'The Rivals – a Tale of the Smart Set' the lines: 'The reunited pair/Were married three weeks later at St

St Peter's, Eaton Square

Peter's, Eaton Square.'

The effigy of George Wilkinson, who was vicar from 1870 to 1883 before becoming Bishop of Truro, is one of the few memorials to survive.

The choir stalls are at the west end, allowing the congregation to feel close to the altar. A professional mixed choir provides music at Sunday's Sung Eucharist. A voluntary choir, with a repertoire from Tallis to Taizé, sings at the earlier family Eucharist. The pure acoustic has led to an annual Eaton Square Concerts autumn series.

Open Monday to Friday (except Wednesday afternoon) 7.30am to 5pm
Eaton Square SW1W 9AL
www.stpetereatonsquare.co.uk

88

St Peter's, London Docks, Limehouse

Anglican

The brick church has a courtyard entrance flanked by clergy and nuns' residencies. The church's architect was Anglo-Catholic supporter Frederick H. Pownall and St Peter's is claimed as one of the first Anglican churches after the Reformation to be built with an interior for catholic worship.

The first vicar was Charles Lowder who, having been heavily influenced at Oxford by Henry Newman, in 1866 opened this church in the riverside part of the St George-in-the-East parish.

One day later cholera was discovered and over the next six weeks the clergy fearlessly ministered to the sick assisted by Sisters of Mercy, led by their founder Elizabeth Neale, sister of hymnwriter J. M. Neale. A tented hospital was erected at the east end of the new church and this work sealed the relationship between church and the docker families.

When Fr Lowder died in 1880 thousands attended the funeral. The south chapel windows depict him twice. Also shown are his successors, Fr Suckling and Fr Alexander Mackonochie. The latter, who faced persecution for upholding catholic liturgy, is shown lying dead in the snow guarded by his faithful dogs.

Also here is Fr Lincoln Wainwright, who came in 1873 as a curate and remained for over 50 years, becoming vicar in 1884. He never had lunch or took a holiday and rarely spent a night away. His blue plaque is on the clergy house. The postwar windows also include the figure of Sister Catherine Elizabeth who died here in the 1940 Blitz.

The main east window is rare in depicting Our Lady of Walsingham. This church has the best examples of stained glass by Margaret Rope, known as Tor, who died in 1988 aged 97. Her windows here, featuring the sacraments, were first in St Augustine, Haggerston.

Pulpits come from St Barnabas, Jericho, in Oxford and St Margaret's Chapel, the forerunner of All Saints Margaret Street. The Lady Chapel reredos features a 1948 painting known as *Our Lady of Wapping* which suggests a desire to confirm this as the special place many locals strongly believed it to be. There are still admiring pilgrims.

The parish is said to run 'from Tower Bridge to the Prospect of Whitby' but Wapping's boundaries were really formed by water with the fiercely independent-

St Peter's, London Docks, Limehouse

minded working-class community able to cut itself off by raising drawbridges against Protestant protesters. Now it is a community that includes immigrants inland and second-home owners on wharves where the smell of spices has evaporated.

Today this is a green church with recycling facilities. It is also a child-friendly church where 'children are welcome all through Mass' and at the Sunday Club. The school is thriving.

There is daily Mass and on Sunday a Solemn Mass and vespers.

Open daily until 6.15pm
Wapping Lane E1W 2RW
www.stpeterslondondocks.org.uk

89
Queen's Chapel of the Savoy, Savoy Hill
Anglican

The narrow St John the Baptist Chapel, wedged in a dark well behind The Savoy, is the sole remains of a hospital founded by Henry VII to provide a night's shelter for homeless men.

'Savoy' recalls Peter of Savoy who was granted the land in 1246 by Henry III. Later it passed to his son, the Earl of Lancaster, and eventually the Duke of Lancaster who became Henry IV. Today the five-acre Precinct of the Savoy is part of the Duchy of Lancaster where the Queen, as Duke of Lancaster, is landlord.

The chapel's gothic reredos by Sidney Smirke includes a fourteenth-century Florentine painting of the Virgin thought to have belonged to the Savoy Hospital. The font was presented by the wife of painter Peter de Wint who is buried in the churchyard. The ceiling is a replica of the Tudor original destroyed by fire in 1864.

Stalls were added in 1937 when George VI made this the Royal Victorian Order's chapel. All recipients have given personal service to the sovereign so the knights' plates include the names and coats of arms of private secretary William Heseltine and solicitor Matthew Farrer.

Arms in the windows include Geoffrey Chaucer whose wedding was in the precinct. Richard D'Oyly Carte, who married here in 1888, is commemorated in one of the few windows to survive World War Two. One window recalls Hugh Chapman, chaplain from 1909 to 1944 and vice-president of the Divorce Reform Union, who welcomed guilty parties seeking remarriage. In *Brideshead Revisited* Evelyn Waugh refers to the Savoy as 'the place where divorced couples got married in those days – a poky little place'. Dr William Cole, master of music from 1954 to 1994, was known to halt an anthem during a fashionable wedding and call for silence if there was chattering.

Orpington's St Olave's School provides a boys' choir. The three-manual Walker organ was presented by the Queen who bears the expenses of the chapel, allowing collections to go to charity.

The Princess Royal attends welcome services for new members of the Royal Victorian Order. The Chancellor of the Duchy of Lancaster, a government minister,

Queen's Chapel of the Savoy, Savoy Hill

is sometimes present at the Duchy Carol Service. The Rogation-tide beating the bounds of the Precinct, including its mid-Thames boundary, has recently been restored.

Sung Eucharist and matins are alternately the main Sunday services when the national anthem is sung with one line changed to 'Long live our noble Duke'.

Open Tuesday to Friday 11.30am to 3.30pm
Savoy Hill WCR2 0DA
www.duchyoflancaster.co.uk

90

St Raphael's, Kingston upon Thames

Roman Catholic

At a distance this Thames riverside building with its square campanile looks like an exaggerated version of an Italian church. It is in fact built of Bath stone but inside this unusual building are gilded Ionian columns and Sicilian marble altar, font and pulpit.

Its history is even more extraordinary for it is a Roman Catholic church erected in 1846 as a private chapel by Alexander Raphael, an Armenian immigrant from India who became an MP and Sheriff of London.

The architect was Charles Parker who had already designed the impressive Unitarian chapel in central London's Stamford Street. Its huge portico survives in front of new flats.

St Raphael's is unexpectedly intimate and narrow inside with grey pillars, cream walls and tall bright windows with pink and blue borders. The French glass is appropriate, for exiled Louis-Philippe attended Mass here. He had fled Paris in the year the church was completed and been given refuge by Queen Victoria at nearby Claremont in Surrey. It was friendship with the French King that brought Chopin to Kingston in Easter Week 1848 when he tested the new organ.

Later, as many as four French royal weddings were held at the church. In 1864 the Count of Paris and the Infanta of Spain, Marie Isabelle, married here. Just over 30 years later they returned for the wedding of their daughter Princess Hélène d'Orléans to Prince Emanuel Duke of Aosta. The church was decorated with palms, orchids and roses and an arch was built over the road. Among the many British royal guests were the then Prince and Princess of Wales. Also represented were the royal houses of Italy, Portugal and Spain.

Alexander Raphael did not live to see the royal events for he died just two years after the chapel had been opened. A nephew inherited the building and opened it to Roman Catholics living in Kingston. Ownership passed to the Earl of Mexborough's family and several are buried in the Savile family crypt along with Alexander Raphael and the first parish priest, John Ainsworth, who served for 30 years.

A memorial on the north wall remembers Princess Anne, a daughter of Lord Mexborough, who died in 1927 attempting to be the first woman to fly the Atlantic from east to west.

St Raphael's, Kingston upon Thames

After World War Two the church was sold to the Archdiocese of Southwark and now it is both a parish church and Kingston University's Roman Catholic chapel.

This small church has a large congregation and even on a winter Saturday morning there can be as many as 30 people at Mass. It is booked at least six months ahead for weddings. Annual events include an outdoor May procession.

On summer Sundays the church can be reached by ferry from the towpath on the far Hampton Court bank.

Open Monday to Friday 9am to 11am
Portsmouth Road KT1 2NA
www.straphael.org.uk

91

Sacred Heart, Wimbledon

Roman Catholic

The Sacred Heart is an exceptionally impressive stone building on high ground seen by commuters on Waterloo trains. Its closeness to the railway is deceptive but from its position on Edge Hill there is a good view across north Surrey. The setting, thanks to a swathe of grass and a mature garden across the road, is unusually pleasant for a suburban location.

It is sometimes suggested that the reason for the 100-foot nave and high roof is that the church was intended to be a cathedral. This is nonsense. The grand construction is entirely due to Edith Arendrup, a member of the wealthy Courtauld family, who moved to nearby Cottenham Park in 1877. Having persuaded the Jesuits at Roehampton to say Mass in her house for her and other local Roman Catholics, she commissioned young Frederick Walters to design a no-expense-spared church. He was an admirer of Pugin and about to embark on a long restoration of Pugin's St George's Cathedral in Southwark.

The Sacred Heart opened in 1887 and was completed, except for a proposed tower which proved too expensive, in 1901. This was long before Walters' work at Southwark was finished.

What gives this church the cathedral-like depth is its ambulatory leading to three chapels including the Lady Chapel. Width is suggested by the addition of the St Ignatius Chapel on the north side paid for by Caroline Currie, sister-in-law of the British Ambassador in Rome. One painting depicts the Jesuit founder begging in England.

Above the nave pillars are statues of Jesuit saints. The high rood screen has figures of Mary, Mary Magdalene and St John based on those found on the rood in St Peter's at Louvain in Belgium. The flanking angels reflect those on the destroyed rood at Westminster Abbey.

A *baldacchino* was removed in 1990 as part of a sanctuary re-ordering which relocated the high altar and its Bentley-designed altar rails. This was sensitively overseen by rector and architectural historian Anthony Symondson. His architect for the controversial changes was Austin Winkley who personally designed the tiled floor.

The new high altar is by David John who included a bronze reliquary underneath containing relics of martyrs Thomas More and Edmund Campion. Victor Galliano,

Sacred Heart, Wimbledon

who worshipped at the church, designed two sanctuary lamp holders.

This is a popular church with around 2,000 people attending on Sunday when there are four morning Masses, including a family one and a Solemn Latin Mass, and two in the evening. Once a month there is an all-night eucharistic adoration.

The Sacred Heart declares itself to be 'a welcoming, open inclusive parish serving the wider community' and a 'church of tomorrow'. It has a huge range of parish organizations, many for young people, and is an active partner in Churches Together. The church benefits from often having priests in residence who are academics from nearby universities.

Open daily when visitors should call at the shop
Edge Hill SW19 4LU
www.sacredheartwimbledon.org.uk

92

St Sepulchre's, Newgate

Anglican

The City's largest church with its 150-foot-high ragstone tower and light airy interior is opposite the Old Bailey.

St Sepulchre-without-Newgate, to give it its full name, stands in the same position in relation to its city as Jerusalem's Church of the Holy Sepulchre – just outside the north-west gate.

The church is first mentioned in 1137 and its tower is fifteenth-century. The nave of the same period was restored rather than redesigned after the Great Fire, but it is to respect Wren's preference for plain glass that a recent offer of seven new stained glass windows by author Patricia Cornwell had to be declined. She wanted to highlight the link with Virginia which is already acknowledged by a window depicting its first governor John Smith, seen holding a map of Virginia, who was saved from death by Princess Pocahontas. Captain Smith is buried in the church.

As at St Andrew's in Holborn, on the far side of the Fleet valley, the churchyard was reduced in size when Holborn Viaduct opened in 1869. Surviving at the north-east corner is the Watch House dating from 1791 which was a guardhouse to deter bodysnatchers intending to sell to nearby St Bart's Hospital.

On the tiny building there is a bust to Charles Lamb who knew the church when he was a pupil at Christ's Hospital which stood opposite. Until recently the school used to return once a year by train from its new home in Sussex for an annual service. By tradition the boys laid bets during the journey on the length of the sermon.

Rector John Rogers, who assisted William Tyndale in translating the Bible into English, was one of the Reformation's Protestant martyrs who died in nearby Smithfield. The church also ministered to Roman Catholic martyrs on their way from Newgate Prison to the Tyburn gallows at the far end of Oxford Street. The Tyburn Walk begins here every April, with prayers for all those who died for their faith in the Tudor years. Both Shakespeare and Dickens refer to the bell sounding for those who had been condemned to death. This may be either the 'Bells of Old Bailey' or the handbell on show which was rung outside the prison cells.

This is the Musicians' Church where the Royal School of Church Music was founded. Stained glass depicts patron saint of music St Cecilia, singer Dame Nellie Melba, and promenade concert founder Sir Henry Wood who was assistant

St Sepulchre's, Newgate

organist at the age of 14. The wreath placed on his bust during the Last Night of the Proms is brought here the following evening to be laid at the burial place of his ashes during a special service.

Choral Evensong is sung every Tuesday and there are lunchtime concerts on Wednesday. There are no Sunday services except on Remembrance Sunday when the Royal Regiment of Fusiliers march here following a wreath-laying at their memorial in Holborn.

Open Monday to Friday
Holborn Viaduct EC1A 2DQ
www.st-sepulchre.org.uk

93
Southwark Cathedral
Anglican

The central London cathedral is London's oldest gothic church and a familiar sight to thousands of commuters who look down from the Charing Cross–London Bridge railway. The fifteenth-century tower rises over Borough Market.

Southwark Cathedral

The dedication is to St Mary Overie, meaning 'over the river' from London, and St Saviour. The first church was probably a Saxon minster which in 1106 became part of an Augustinian priory. One of the oldest visible parts is the retro-choir dating from the year of Magna Carta, 1215.

The nave was rebuilt in the nineteenth century and here in a splendid tomb is John Gower who appears in William Shakespeare's play *Pericles*. His brother Edmund Shakespeare, an actor, is buried in the choir along with dramatists John Fletcher and Philip Massinger. Bishop Lancelot Andrewes, who worked on the Authorized Version of the Bible, lies near the high altar.

William Shakespeare has his own memorial where he lies in effigy, often clutching a fresh sprig of thyme. The window above features characters from his plays and a modern tablet alongside recalls Sam Wanamaker who rebuilt the nearby Globe.

In 1607 the playwright probably attended the baptism of John Harvard who has given his name not just to a university but to a chapel here that has a tall Pugin tabernacle.

Just inside the main cathedral entrance and in front of Norman arcading is a memorial to those drowned in 1989 when the *Marchioness* sank in the Thames.

Weddings include James I of Scotland to Joan, a lady-in-waiting to Henry V's Queen, at Candlemas in 1423. Her uncle Cardinal Beaufort presided at St Joan of Arc's trial and his shield can be found in the south transept. In 2008 Rolling Stone Ronnie Wood gave away his daughter at a star-studded wedding.

When the priory closed in 1539 its church became the parish church. Although

Tomb of John Gower in Southwark Cathedral

cathedral status was conferred in 1905 this remains Southwark's parish church with the offices of IPC magazines and the *Financial Times* within the boundary, along with the Menier Chocolate Factory as well as many flats and houses.

The Queen came to give thanks on Millennium Eve before going downriver to the Dome, and a few years later Her Majesty returned secretly to record her Christmas Day message. In 2006 she unveiled the Mohegan Indian memorial in the churchyard. Her daughter-in-law, the Duchess of Wessex, is patron of the Cathedral Friends.

In 2001 Nelson Mandela opened new buildings which include a refectory and library.

The cathedral's Greater Choir which sings at festivals is formed by the boys', girls' and men's choirs. A third of the packed Sunday congregation is local. Our Lady's Birthday and Christ the King are kept as patronal festivals.

Other annual events include the blessing of the Thames on the Baptism of Our Lord and tower-top singing on Ascension Day. Many bishops come here for their consecration and students for their graduation. There are weekly organ and classical recitals.

Open daily
London Bridge SE1 9DA
www.southwarkcathedral.org.uk

94

Stanmore Old Church

Anglican

The roofless brick St John's Church stands on slightly higher ground than the Victorian replacement alongside. Inside the nave is blocked by a tomb but the west windows frame the new church.

A Saxon church, St Mary's, stood over half a mile to the south but as the village centre moved it was decided to erect its successor, St John's, on this site. It was built in 1632, paid for by merchant adventurer Sir John Wolstenholme. The Bishop of London William Laud came to consecrate it and found this action quoted against him at his trial 13 years later as the Puritans gained power. Laud's reply was that 'Stanmore was no chapel but a true parish church'.

By 1845 the church had become too small for expanding Stanmore which was now served by the railway. In 1850 a third church was built in the field next door. This was gothic style with Kentish ragstone. Former Chancellor of the Exchequer and Foreign Secretary Lord Aberdeen, soon to be Prime Minister, laid the foundation stone in the presence of William IV's widow, Queen Adelaide, who was making her last public appearance.

The old church had been sold to the builders of the new but when the roof was removed there was an outcry which halted demolition. The much loved building remains open air but still consecrated and used for occasional services. Bishop David Hope presided at one in 1992 and every year the Easter Vigil begins here.

After being a picturesque ruin for a century it was listed as an important example of Stuart brickwork. In 1991 a fox seen disappearing into a hole led the verger to discover a vault containing the coffin of Lord Aberdeen complete with a coronet resting on top.

Memorials remaining include some to the Drummond family of Drummond's Bank. At the east end are buried Sir John Wolstenholme and his father who were brought from St Mary's.

Both churches have battlemented towers. The font, the last work of royal master mason Nicholas Stone, has been moved from the old to the new church. Its Victorian interior was re-ordered and the walls whitewashed in the 1960s. More recently it has been considered a typical enough London church to be used twice in episodes of television's *EastEnders*.

The new church was known to W. S. Gilbert of Gilbert and Sullivan fame who

Stanmore Old Church

is buried just outside the south-west corner. Other burials in the large churchyard include Shakespeare's nephew and heir William Hart, who acted with the King's Men, and Lord Chancellor Lord Halsbury who is known for *Halsbury's Laws of England* digest which was first published in 1907.

Edward Carpenter was rector until parishioner Clement Attlee recommended him for Westminster Abbey where eventually he became dean.

'New' St John's is a popular church for weddings especially as there is a mock medieval church hall, complete with baronial fireplace and a minstrels gallery, for the reception.

The old church is open Saturdays from April to September 2.30pm to 4.30pm
Church Road HA7 4AQ
www.stjohnsstanmore.org.uk

95
St Stephen's, Gloucester Road
Anglican

The stone church, on the corner of Gloucester Road and Southwell Gardens, is surrounded by much taller houses and flats which often leave the church garden with its palm tree in the shade. The brick interior is painted a warm but subtle red.

The first St Stephen's was an iron mission church opened in 1863 on a site opposite the future Gloucester Road Station. Within three years the present building designed by Joseph Peacock was ready to welcome those moving into the new terraces.

The stained glass windows depicting the major saints on each side of the nave date from just after this period when the church had fallen under the influence of the Oxford Movement. By the turn of the century the interior had begun more and more to reflect this change. A reredos by G. F. Bodley was added in 1903 and a rood screen by Walter Tapper in 1908.

The deep blue and red east window high above the altar is by John Hayward and was added in 1962. The statue of St Stephen was erected in memory of Fr Eric Cheetham whose long period as vicar from 1929 to 1956 included difficult war years when he ministered to those sheltering in the Underground station. He first came to the church as curate to his predecessor Revd the Lord Victor Seymour, the youngest of the Marquess of Hertford's ten children, who had been appointed in 1900 and knew G. F. Bodley.

A plaque by the statue of Our Lady remembers the poet T. S. Eliot who was churchwarden for a quarter of a century. He had been introduced to the church in 1933 by Fr Cheetham. The following year Eliot became, without ever facing election, churchwarden, and only stepped down in 1959 although he continued to worship here until his death in 1965. His poetry proved to be an influence on Gyles Brandreth who, as a boy altar server, met the poet.

The church remains a leading catholic Anglican church with the centre of its common life being the Solemn Mass on Sunday morning. There is also daily Mass.

In 2009, former vicar Christopher Colven became rector of St James's, Spanish Place, having resigned to become a Roman Catholic when the Church of England agreed to ordain women. Those remaining at St Stephen's have placed themselves

St Stephen's, Gloucester Road

under the jurisdiction of the Bishop of Fulham who looks after those London churches unwilling to be served by women priests.

There is a high standard of liturgy and music. The Guild of All Souls, founded in 1873 and patron of the church, holds its annual requiem here. There is a crowded congregation of visitors on Boxing Day morning for the church's patronal festival.

Rush hour recitals on Monday evenings and regular Thursday concerts attract those who are away at weekends. Each May an arts and faith festival brings visitors from across the capital.

Open Monday to Friday (except Wednesday) 8.30am to 2pm
Southwell Gardens SW7 4RL
www.saint-stephen.org.uk

96
St Stephen, Walbrook
Anglican

This is the Lord Mayor's church behind Mansion House but its rough exterior is a reminder that it was not intended to be seen without adjoining buildings. Now built into a corner is a Starbucks and alongside covered steps lead up to the church entrance.

The interior has a central altar and is free of pews which allows an appreciation of this unusual Wren church described by Sir John Betjeman as 'a plain rectangle

St Stephen, interior

. . . full of vistas'. Sir John Summerson thought it 'one of the few City churches in which the genius of Wren shines in full splendour'. But the greatest praise came earlier from the eighteenth-century Italian sculptor Canova who said: 'We have nothing to touch it in Rome.' Nikolaus Pevsner ranked it among London's ten most important buildings, even though he was writing before the re-ordering.

The first church on the site, replacing a Saxon one nearby, was built in 1428 with the assistance of the Duke of Bedford. After this was destroyed in the 1666 Great Fire rebuilding started as early as 1672, probably as this was Wren's own parish church where he could have a free hand. It is a lesson in geometry and a trial run for the St Paul's Cathedral he really wanted with a proportionally larger dome. The new St Stephen's opened in 1679 although the steeple was not completed until 1717.

Dominant today is the eight-ton central altar made by Henry Moore. Before being brought here it stood among cows in a Hertfordshire field, while critics, who likened the stone to a 'ripe camembert cheese', forced a rare sitting of the Court

St Stephen, Walbrook

of Ecclesiastical Causes Reserved. Patrick Heron designed the curving cushion kneelers around the altar.

This dramatic rearrangement was masterminded by the churchwarden Lord Palumbo who stored his wine in the crypt. He also saved the church from the damp said to maybe come from the Walbrook stream. The rector at this time was Chad Varah who had been appointed in 1953 and stayed for 50 years. He called himself the first sex therapist when founding the Samaritans, using a telephone still found at the back of the church.

Early visitors, when there was still a Sunday service, included the Brontë sisters. They came in 1848 hoping to hear the rector Dr George Croly preach but were disappointed.

Composer John Dunstaple, who died on Christmas Eve 1453, was buried in the old church. Here in an unmarked grave is Wren's young colleague, the architect Sir John Vanbrugh. More recent funerals include Marcus Morris, founder of *Eagle* comic, who had once employed Chad Varah.

Lady Sarah Armstrong-Jones' wedding in 1994 brought her royal relatives to the church including her mother Princess Margaret and aunt Elizabeth II.

This is the base for London's Internet Church. On Thursdays a consort of four singers provide an unaccompanied Mass setting, often seventeenth-century, for the lunchtime Choral Eucharist and on Fridays there is a lunchtime organ recital. There is no Sunday service.

Open daily Monday to Friday
Walbrook EC4 8BN
www.ststephenwalbrook.net; www.londoninternetchurch.org.uk

97

Temple Church, Fleet Street
Anglican

The partly round lawyers' church is found suddenly after turning a corner in the lanes of The Temple off Fleet Street.

It was built by 1185 for the Knights Templar and consecrated by the Patriarch of Jerusalem. The nave is round to reflect the Holy Sepulchre in Jerusalem which the Knights were protecting. Like the original round building covering Christ's empty tomb, this replica also has a conventional hall shape extension for worship.

The Knights Templar was dissolved by the King of France on Friday 13 October 1307, which forever made any Friday the 13th allegedly unlucky. At The Temple the chaplain's official title remains that of the medieval English head of the knights: the Reverend and Valiant Master of the Temple.

Eight of the warrior monks lie in the round in effigy. Some have their legs crossed which is not so much a code for having been on a crusade as a sign of a knight's readiness for action. Two knights are over six feet tall which means that when mounted in armour they would have been a formidable enemy. The figures, once painted, were damaged by a World War Two incendiary bomb but fortunately casts had been taken for the 1851 Great Exhibition.

In 1608 James I gave the precinct to the lawyers who had been there for several generations. This is now the Inner and Middle Temple, the former being the nearest to the City. The boundary runs down the centre of the church with the north being for the Middle and the south for the Inner. For a time there were rival organs maintained on each side of the building.

Christopher Wren, who was married here, gave the east end a classical look which survived until the Victorians ripped it out in 1840. The present reredos was banished to Bowes Museum which saved it from destruction in the Blitz.

After the war the Purbeck columns in the choir had to be replaced but the new ones have been made to lean like the old ones. Carl Edwards designed the glass in the east window and in 2008 his daughter was responsible for The Temple's 400th anniversary window on the south side.

Today there are 18 boy choristers. Handel often visited to hear John Stanley, the nearly blind composer and organist, who was known as a brilliant harpsichord player. In 1844 Edward Hopkins gave the first organ performance of Mendelssohn's *Wedding March*. Hopkins was the organist for 55 years but George Thalben-Ball

Temple Church, Fleet Street

was organist for 58 years and one of his choristers was Ernest Lough who in 1927 recorded 'O, for the wings of a dove'. The disc sold a million copies and attracted so many to evensong that tickets had to be issued.

Many of today's visitors come because they have read about the church in *The Da Vinci Code* which the Master welcomes as a mission opportunity.

The main Sunday service is either Choral Matins or Choral Eucharist.

Open most afternoons
Temple EC4Y 7BB
www.templechurch.com

98

Tyburn Chapel, Marble Arch

Roman Catholic

The chapel, on the noisy main road by Marble Arch, has a modern nondescript frontage as a result of wartime bombing.

It is part of the convent of the Benedictine Adorers of the Sacred Heart of Jesus of Montmartre, better known as the Tyburn Nuns, who keep alive the memory of

Site of the Tyburn gallows

Roman Catholic martyrs who died close by at the Tyburn gallows. The spot is marked in the ground on the traffic island at the Oxford Street–Edgware Road junction. A triangular structure allowed for three people to be hanged, drawn and quartered together.

The name comes from the River Tyburn, whose valley is discernible in Oxford Street, and the also hidden Tyburn Brook flowing to the west and feeding the Westbourne.

In 1535 St John Houghton, Prior of Charterhouse, was hanged along with St Augustine Webster, St Robert Lawrence, St Richard Reynolds of Syon and Blessed John Haile of Isleworth. In 1581 St Edmund Campion prayed on the scaffold for those responsible for his death 'that we may at last be friends in heaven, when all injuries shall be forgotten'.

William Shakespeare is thought to have been in the crowd when his priest friend Robert Dibdale was killed in 1595. The last martyr to be brought here was St Oliver Plunket in 1681.

In 1585 Fr Gregory Gunn predicted that a convent would be built where Edmund Campion died and he and others are remembered today at the convent which has some relics. The chapel stands on the site of 7 Hyde Park Place, once home of Tractarian James Hope-Scott who was visited by Henry Newman.

Marie Adele Garnier brought her small community of nuns from Paris in 1903. She had founded the Benedictine order in 1901 on Montmartre 'to glorify the Most Blessed Trinity'. Tyburn is now the mother house of convents in Ireland, Scotland, Australia, New Zealand, Peru, Ecuador and Colombia. In 2005 another opened in Rome.

Tyburn Chapel, Marble Arch

This is an enclosed order rarely seen outside except on polling day. The sisters enjoy fresh air and sport in their hidden garden.

After World War Two damage, the chapel was not rebuilt until 1962, with additions in 1991. Architect F. G. Broadbent worked to designs by Goodhart-Rendel. The church, which adjoins the convent, is a reversed L with a white interior. The nave is divided from the sanctuary by a screen, like a prison cage. The community sits in the half-hidden choir on the north side. The focus is the Blessed Sacrament in the monstrance above a stone altar, and between services there is, day and night, a sister keeping the perpetual adoration.

The sisters pray for the canonization of their foundress Mother Marie Adele Garnier who died here in 1924. Every spring the Tyburn Walk, which traces the Reformation martyrs' last journey from Newgate Prison via St Giles-in-the-Fields to Tyburn, ends in front of the chapel with Benediction given from the balcony.

Open 6.30am to 8.30pm
Hyde Park Place, Marble Arch W2 2LJ
www.tyburnconvent.org.uk

99
St Vedast, Foster Lane
Anglican

The small church in narrow Foster Lane can be glimpsed behind a new building set back from the corner of Cheapside. Glass doors allow passers-by to look directly into the church which resembles a college chapel. This is the work of Stephen Dykes Bower who re-ordered the church after its near destruction in the World War Two blitz.

There has been a church on this site since 1249 and its rare dedication to St Vedast, better known in Belgium, may suggest that there was a Flemish community in this part of the City.

This London church was rebuilt after the Great Fire under Christopher Wren's direction on the old foundation between 1695 and 1712 when the steeple was added. The south wall retains some medieval work. But Wren cleverly disguised the irregular ground plan as an oblong.

Incumbents include Thomas Rotherham who, under Edward IV, became Lord Chancellor and Archbishop of York. Thomas Pelham Dale was appointed in 1847 as an evangelical but at Christmas 1873 he introduced vestments, much to the annoyance of a churchwarden. This was soon followed by lighted candles and Gregorian chant. Relations worsened when in 1875 he supported Fr Mackonochie of St Alban's in Holborn in his struggle to maintain catholic traditions. Dale found himself referred to the Court of Arches and then suddenly arrested. His incarceration in Holloway Prison and his dramatic release on Christmas Eve 1880 won him huge public sympathy.

In 1947 writer and journalist Bernard Mortlock was appointed priest of the bombed church and, while the building was restored, he found replacement furnishings from churches not being rebuilt. The altar and royal arms are from St Matthew Friday Street, the reredos from St Christopher le Stocks, the organ case from St Bartholomew-by-the-Exchange and the pulpit from All Hallows Bread Street.

The rectory, replacing a pub, was the first postwar house to be built in the City, and when later Canon Mortlock became Canon Treasurer of Chichester Cathedral he stayed on as rector so as to retain use of the town house. He was a friend of Epstein whose stone relief of the rector is in the tiny cloister. The rectory has a Hans Feibusch mural.

St Vedast, Foster Lane

Later this was the home of Gonville ffrench-Beytagh who, when Dean of Johannesburg, had been imprisoned and deported for his anti-apartheid stance. His appointment to St Vedast provided a home and base for his continuing support for the oppressed in South Africa.

The neighbouring Goldsmiths' Company comes to worship on St Dunstan's Day, bringing their own chalice. Robert Herrick, a goldsmith's son who chronicled the liturgical year, was baptized here in 1591. The church maintains the catholic tradition established at such cost by Thomas Dale as well as a high standard of music. There is a daily lunchtime Mass. St Vedast Day on 6 February is observed with a crowded festival Mass.

Open Monday to Friday
Foster Lane EC2V 6HH
www.vedast.net

100

Wesley's Chapel, City Road
Methodist

The mother church of Methodism stands in an eighteenth-century courtyard just outside the City and opposite leafy Bunhill Fields. This simple, light chapel is now darkened by rich stained glass and walls heavy with memorials.

Once damp ground here was made firm by soil excavated from the site of Wren's St Paul's Cathedral. The chapel's architect, who is buried in St Paul's, was George Dance the Younger who had just redesigned All Hallows London Wall. His Methodist church was opened in 1778 by founder John Wesley after George III had given masts from old warships to support the gallery. At the time the building had the largest unsupported ceiling in the country.

The dominant 10-foot-high pulpit has been cut down from its original 15 feet. When Wesley's brother Charles preached, the person below once caught a falling Bible dislodged by the exuberant speaker. Although central, the pulpit is rare in having a space at its base to allow a view of the communion table behind. John Wesley believed in word and sacrament.

Memorials include one to William Morley Punshon who was as famous in Canada as England and raised money for churches in growing seaside towns. A modern window by Mark Cazalet called 'God as Fire' commemorates World Methodist Council chairman Donald English.

The altar rail is the gift of Lady Thatcher who was married here and brought her children Mark and Carol to be baptized here.

The Foundery Chapel contains benches from the chapel in the original headquarters about 200 yards to the south in a former arms factory.

In 1978, 200 years to the day after the chapel opened, the Queen came to a re-opening which followed a huge restoration funded by Methodists around the world. Demolition had been considered on the basis that Methodists should invest in mission not buildings but when American Methodists offered to buy the chapel it was agreed to launch an appeal. Upkeep is now partly funded by an office block on a narrow strip of land at the back. Its reflective glass is the backdrop to the tomb of John Wesley.

He lived in the next-door house, a rare Georgian survival built a year after the chapel opened, where he rose daily at 4am. He died at home there in 1791. His hymn-writer brother Charles stayed regularly on the third floor. From the

Wesley's Chapel, City Road

windows can be seen Bunhill Fields where their mother Susanna is buried.

Wesley's successors at the 'Methodist cathedral' are often well known and include broadcaster Dr Colin Morris who was minister here from 1969 to 1973. In 1996 another broadcaster Dr Leslie Griffiths became the superintendent minister.

A museum in the crypt tells the story of both the chapel and worldwide Methodism. The congregation has recently grown and is always swollen on Sunday by visitors from around the world and especially countries such as the USA where Methodism has a greater following than in the UK.

The church and house are open Monday to Saturday 10am to 4pm
City Road EC1Y 1AU
www.wesleyschapel.org.uk

Bibliography

Amery, Colin, *St George's, Bloomsbury*, World Monuments Fund, 2008.

Bradley, Simon and Pevsner, Nikolaus, *The Buildings of England, London 1: The City of London*, Penguin, 1997.

Bradley, Simon and Pevsner, Nikolaus, *The Buildings of England, London 6: Westminster*, Yale, 2003.

Cherry, Bridget and Pevsner, Nikolaus, *The Buildings of England, London 2: South*, Penguin, 1983.

Cherry, Bridget and Pevsner, Nikolaus, *The Buildings of England, London 3: North West*, Penguin, 1991.

Cherry, Bridget and Pevsner, Nikolaus, *The Buildings of England, London 4: North*, Penguin, 1999.

Day, Hermitage and Ellwood G. M., *Some London Churches*, Mowbray, 1911.

Hibbert, Christopher, *London's Churches*, Queen Anne Press, 1988.

Humphrey, Stephen, *Churches and Cathedrals of London*, New Holland, 2000.

Jeffrey, Paul, *The City Churches of Sir Christopher Wren*, Hambledon Press, 1996.

Jeffrey, Paul, *The Parish Church of St Mary-at-Hill in the City of London*, Ecclesiological Society, 1996.

Jenkins, Simon, *England's Thousand Best Churches*, Penguin, 2000.

Kendall, Derek, *City of London Churches: A Pictorial Rediscovery*, Collins & Brown, 1998.

Martin, Christopher, *A Glimpse of Heaven*, English Heritage, 2006.

Middleton, Paul and Hatts, Leigh, *London City Churches*, Bankside Press, 2003.

Tames, Richard, *The Westminster & Pimlico Book*, Historical Publications, 2005.

Weinreb, Ben and Hibbert, Christopher, *The London Encyclopaedia*, Macmillan, 1995.

Yates, Nigel, *Anglican Ritualism in Victorian Britain 1830–1910*, Clarendon Press, 2000.

Index of Names and Subjects

Index of Churches Not in the Main Listing